THE CHARLES DICKENS SHOW

THE CHARLES DICKENS SHOW

An Account of his Public Readings
1858–1870

by

RAYMUND FITZSIMONS

PUBLISHED BY

GEOFFREY BLES · LONDON

1970

© RAYMUND FITZSIMONS, 1970

Printed in Great Britain
by Cox & Wyman Ltd, Fakenham

SBN: 7138 0282 0

Published by
GEOFFREY BLES LTD
52 Doughty Street, London, WC1N 2LZ
36–38 Clarence Street, Sydney, N.S.W. 2000
353 Elizabeth Street, Melbourne, C.1.
246 Queen Street, Brisbane
CML Building, King William Street, Adelaide, S.A. 5000
Lake Road, Northcote, Auckland
100 Lesmill Road, Don Mills, Ontario
P.O. Box 8879, Johannesburg
P.O. Box 834, Cape Town
P.O. Box 2800, Salisbury, Rhodesia

TO
MY SON
JAMES

... "Ride on! Rough-shod if need be, smooth-shod if that will do, but ride on! Ride on over all obstacles, and win the race!"

"And win what race?" said I.

"The race that one has started in," said he. "Ride on!"

I noticed, I remember, as he paused, looking at me with his handsome head a little thrown back, and his glass raised in his hand, that, though the freshness of the sea-wind was on his face, and it was ruddy, there were traces in it, made since I last saw it, as if he had applied himself to some habitual strain of the fervent energy which, when roused, was so passionately roused within him ...

David Copperfield

Contents

Illustrations

[1] Radio Times, Hulton Picture Library
[2] Raymond Mander and Joe Mitchenson Theatre Collection

Acknowledgements

The author is grateful to the Nonesuch Press for permission to quote from *The Letters of Charles Dickens*, edited by Walter Dexter; to the Henry W. and Albert A. Berg Collection, New York Public Library, for permission to reproduce a page of Dickens's prompt copy of *Mrs. Gamp;* to John Greaves, Honorary Secretary of The Dickens Fellowship, for his help in locating illustrations; and to Anne Fitzsimons for compiling the total number of Readings given by Dickens.

INTRODUCTION

The Public Readings of Charles Dickens were the greatest one-man show of the nineteenth century. "Dickens is coming!" was the ecstatic shout in towns where he was announced to read. In London the cheers that greeted his appearance on the platform could be heard a block away. In Edinburgh he had to calm a rioting audience. In Glasgow the audience tried to storm the platform and carry him away. In Boston, New York and Philadelphia people queued for tickets all night in temperatures well below freezing point.

The excesses of his public would today be more associated with a pop star than a writer reading extracts from his own works. Yet, in the true sense of the term, Dickens was a pop star, one of the greatest of all time. He was the most popular author in the English-speaking world. His books had sounded a response in the hearts of his readers and through them countless people had come to love him. The Readings appealed, as did the books, to all ages and to all tastes, cultivated and simple. It was this universal appeal that put the Readings into a different category from all other entertainments.

For the Readings were an entertainment. They were not readings in the literal sense of the word. Dickens was a magnificent actor, with a wonderful talent for mimicry. He seemed able to alter not only his voice, his features and his carriage but also his stature. He disappeared and the audience saw, as the case might be, Fagin, Scrooge, Pickwick, Mrs. Gamp, Squeers, Mrs. Gummidge, Micawber, Bill Sikes, or a host of others. Character after character appeared on the platform, living and breathing in the flesh.

Dickens began reading professionally at a time when his literary powers were declining. His marriage was in ruins and he had taken a young mistress, Ellen Ternan. He was restless and deeply unhappy. He believed that reading would bring him the distraction he sought and also provide him with an alternative livelihood if his literary talent were to fail him. In Britain and America he was brought face to face with multitudes of his readers and he realised for the first time the full extent of his fame. His audiences showed their love for him every time he appeared on the platform. Ordinary people would stop him in the street to thank him for all the pleasure he had given them.

The Readings came to mean so much to him that he could not live without them. Only on the platform, under the hot bright lights, with an audience in front of him, could he feel himself again vibrating with his old zest for living. No other pursuit could keep at bay his ever-lengthening moods of depression. The Readings distracted him from the thoughts on which he was constantly brooding: the degradation of his childhood; the failing of his literary powers; the separation from his sons; the decline of his superhuman energy and the approach of old age. The "Murder" Reading, especially, became for him a means of expressing all the things he raged against in his mind. As the ferocious blows rained down on the imaginary upturned face of Nancy, he was, perhaps, symbolically enacting his bitterness for his wife and his guilt over Ellen Ternan.

Nothing could stop him from reading, not even bad health and the warnings of his doctors. During the last three years of his life, this great literary genius barnstormed across Britain and America in a series of one-night stands, dragging himself to the reading desk when he was scarcely fit enough to stand. Driven by his unhappiness and his need of an audience, he hurried from town to town, until, worn out by his exertions, he vanished from "these garish lights for ever more" three months before his death.

have never done it in public, though I have in private, and (if I may say so) with a great effect on the hearers." He had first read the *Carol* ten years previously to a group of friends at John Forster's chambers in Lincoln's Inn. The following year he read *The Chimes* to Macready, the actor. He told his wife: "If you had seen Macready last night – undisguisedly sobbing and crying on the sofa, as I read – you would have felt (as I did) what a thing it is to have power."

When Dickens appeared on the platform, the audience were not certain what he was going to do. A "Reading" sounded dull and most of them had braved the weather simply to look at the famous author. Even those who had seen him act in the same hall some eighteen months previously, when he brought his amateur company to Birmingham, were not prepared for an evening of theatrical excitements. When the applause that greeted his appearance had died away, Dickens opened his book and began to read.

"A Christmas Carol in four staves. Stave one, Marley's Ghost. Marley was dead to begin with. There was no doubt whatever about that." The opening sentences were spoken in cheerful tones. "The register of his burial was signed by the clergyman, the clerk, the undertaker, and the chief mourner. Scrooge signed it, and Scrooge's name was good upon 'Change, for anything he chose to put his hand to. *Oh! but he was a tight-fisted hand at the grindstone, Scrooge!*" The voice had changed. The description of the miser – "a squeezing, wrenching, grasping, scraping, clutching, covetous old sinner" – was eliminated from the Reading. There was no need for it; Scrooge himself was standing on the platform.

From that moment onwards, Dickens had the audience in the palm of his hand. He roused them to terror with the clanking approach of the *thing*, which came nearer and nearer to the door of Scrooge's room. "Upon its coming in" – and here his voice rose with startling effect – "the dying flame leaped up as though it cried, 'I know him! Marley's Ghost!' and fell again." Immediately after this he had them laughing at the macabre humour of

Scrooge, who, peering at the ghost of his old partner and observing it to be so transparent that he could see the two back buttons on the coat behind, reflected that "he had often heard Marley spoken of as having no bowels, but had never believed it until then." He made them cry when he spoke of Bob Cratchit describing his little boy's grave and breaking down in an agony of weeping. "He broke down all at once. He couldn't help it," Dickens said. Then added in a low voice, "If he could have helped it, he and his child would have been further apart than they were."

The moods of the Reading changed so rapidly that the audience had scarcely time to dry their eyes before they were enjoying the fun of Scrooge's discovery of Christmas Day and his conversation with the boy in the court below about purchasing the prize turkey at the near-by poulterer's shop. This was followed by the gaiety of the party at the home of Scrooge's nephew and the arrival of the regenerated Scrooge. "Will you let me in, Fred?" "*Let him in!*" All the cordiality and goodwill of Christmas were in the voice and face of Dickens. "*It's a wonder he didn't shake his arm off!*"

When the Reading ended the audience sat radiant and smiling. Then they went out into the dark rain-swept streets of Birmingham, knowing that even in this world there really were such things as goodness, love, peace and forgiveness.

Two nights later, in the same hall, Dickens read another of his Christmas stories, *The Cricket on the Hearth*. These Readings were such a sensation that he was asked to give a second Reading of the *Carol* on the 30th. He agreed to do this if the greater part of the seating accommodation was made available to working people at reduced prices. They proved to be the finest audience of the three. He wrote: "They lost nothing, misinterpreted nothing, followed everything closely, laughed and cried with the most delightful earnestness, and animated me to that extent that I felt as if we were all bodily going up into the clouds together."

Dickens had always loved the stimulus of an audience and had he not become a writer he would have certainly become an actor.

His view of life was theatrical. With him the most trifling conversation was a little acted drama taking place behind the glare of footlights. The conventions of the theatre dictated the structure of his novels. Shorn of their humour and ironical comment, the framework and situations are melodramatic. This is why so many of his books were adapted for the Victorian stage. Eight versions of *The Cricket on the Hearth* were produced in London theatres within a year of its publication in 1845.

He had been obsessed by the theatre from his earliest years. When he was about six years old he was taken to the Theatre Royal, Rochester, where he saw *Richard III* and also *Macbeth*. Two years later he was brought up to London for a Christmas pantomime and saw the great clown, Joseph Grimaldi, at whom he clapped his hands "with great precocity". There was no theatre-going during those dark months of his childhood spent in Warren's Blacking Factory, but when the family fortunes revived and he was sent to Wellington House Academy, he took a leading part in the school theatricals. While working as an office boy in Doctor's Commons, he went to the theatre almost every night. As a parliamentary reporter, he went as often as the evening debates allowed. In those days he looked and dressed like an actor: slender, elegant and dandified, his delicate features framed with long silky brown hair. What Vincent Crummles said of Nicholas Nickleby could also be said of Dickens: "There's genteel comedy in your walk and manner; juvenile tragedy in your eye, and touch-and-go farce in your laugh."

In 1832, when he was twenty years old, he thought seriously of becoming an actor and applied for an audition at the Lyceum Theatre. "I wrote to Bartley, who was stage manager, and told him how young I was and exactly what I thought I could do, and that I believed I had a strong perception of character and oddity, and a natural power of reproducing in my own person what I observed in others." Bartley offered him an audition, but on the day Dickens was laid up with a bad cold and inflammation of the face. He told Bartley that he would resume his application the following season, but by then he had made a great reputation as a newspaper reporter and had left off thinking of becoming a professional actor.

But his obsession with the theatre continued. Again and again, throughout his career, he turned from writing to acting. Amateur theatricals were a passion with him. During his hectic American trip in 1842 he found time to produce three plays with the officers of the Montreal garrison. He not only directed the plays but also acted in all three of them. In 1845 he brought together a distinguished group of amateurs and presented Ben Jonson's *Every Man in His Humour* at the Royalty Theatre. He gave a bravura performance as Captain Bobadil and three years later scored another success as Justice Shallow in *The Merry Wives of Windsor*. All who saw him agreed that he was a great actor, from drama critics to the stage carpenter who told him with unconscious irony, "It's a universal observation in the profession, sir, that it was a great loss to the public when you took to writing books."

The Birmingham Readings gave him another opportunity to indulge his passion for acting, but he welcomed them not only for this but also because they came at a time when he was seeking distractions of any kind. In December 1853, when he read at Birmingham, he was restless and unhappy. At forty-one he already considered himself middle-aged. He was conscious of a decline in his superhuman energy and he dreaded the prospect of old age. He had recently completed *Bleak House* and for the first time in his life he had experienced difficulty in finishing a book. Up to the completion of *David Copperfield* three years previously, he was confident that his powers of invention were inexhaustible, but during the writing of the final part of *Bleak House* he had had to face the thought that what had been his greatest talent might some day fail him. He could not settle to writing another book. Every day he went for a long walk of twelve miles or so, striding along like a madman, trying to thrash things out in his mind. Some nights he went with his bohemian friends on sybaritic excursions to the green rooms of London theatres, seeking the company of young actresses and ballet girls.

He knew these distractions were having an unfavourable effect on his work, but he could see no way out of his situation. He sometimes thought of going away from everyone, to write a book in solitude, perhaps in the Pyrénées, or in some Swiss monastery above the snowline. In 1854 he wrote to John Forster: "*Restlessness*, you will say. Whatever it is, it is always driving me, and I cannot help it. I have rested nine or ten weeks, and sometimes feel as if it had been a year – though I had the strangest nervous miseries before I stopped. If I couldn't walk fast and far, I should just explode and perish." He made an allusion to the kind of experience he had described in *David Copperfield:* "the so happy and yet so unhappy existence which seeks its realities in unrealities, and finds its dangerous comfort in a perpetual escape from the disappointment of heart around it." He asked Forster: "Why is it, that as with poor David, a sense comes always crushing on me now, when I fall into low spirits, as of one happiness I have missed in life, and one friend and companion I have never made."

He was deeply unhappy in his marriage. His wife's inability to share in his work had always distressed him and he believed that in this crisis she had failed him once again. When he had married Catherine he was in love with her. She was the daughter of George Hogarth, editor of the *Evening Chronicle*, and he was a reporter with a brilliant reputation. They were a contrasted pair. She was voluptuous and indolent; he was eager and restless. She was devoted and unenterprising; he was intense and ambitious. Her eyes were somnolent; his shone with intellect and humour. His whole person spoke life and action, and beside his face every other face seemed dead.

They were married in 1836, when he was twenty-four years old and she was twenty. She was soon complaining that his long hours as a reporter kept him from her, but he would not alter his way of life to suit her. During their courtship he had charted all her moods and he let her know the ones she must not indulge at his expense.

Yet in the early days they were happy enough. The year of their marriage was the year of *Pickwick Papers*. Every class of society, from the highest to the lowest, followed the adventures of Mr. Pickwick, month by month, with shouts of laughter, and by the end of the year Dickens had become the most popular writer in the country.

In the years that followed he was lionised wherever he went. He usually went alone, because Catherine, more often than not, was obliged by pregnancy or the needs of their growing family to stay at home. He was handsome and gallant, as well as famous, and he often sought out the company of some pretty young girl with whom he could enjoy an emotional but innocent relationship. He knew that Catherine was jealous and this annoyed him, not only because he believed her jealousy to be unjustified but because he could not bear the thought of anyone sitting in judgement on him.

Whenever she did take part in his social life, she was neither a good hostess nor a good guest. She had little conversation and she did not shine in company. Her lack of social graces irritated him as did her physical clumsiness. During the American trip in 1842, he wrote half-jokingly to Forster: "She falls into, and out of, every coach or boat we enter; scrapes the skin off her legs; brings great sores and swellings on her feet; chips large fragments out of her ankle-bones; and makes herself blue with bruises." In 1845 he parodied her in *The Cricket on the Hearth* as Tilly Slowboy, the great clumsy nursemaid.

By 1850 their marriage had failed. During this year he was writing *David Copperfield* and some hint of his situation is given in the chapters that deal with David's married life. David speaks of an old unhappy feeling, "like a strain of sorrowful music faintly heard in the night," that there was always something wanting, something missing. "What I missed, I still regarded – I always regarded – as something that had been a dream of my youthful fancy; that was incapable of realisation; that I was now discovering to be so, with some natural pain, as all men did. But that it would have been better if my wife could have helped me more, and shared the many thoughts in which I had no partner; and that this might have been; I knew." Again a hint of his thoughts is given in the melancholy refrain that is heard throughout these chapters: "There can be no disparity in marriage like unsuitability of mind and purpose."

During these months he indulged in amateur theatricals more than ever. In 1850 three performances of *Every Man in His Humour* were given at Lord Lytton's home at Knebworth. Dickens had long cherished the idea of a society for the benefit of impoverished authors, and at Knebworth the Guild of Literature and Art was inaugurated. Funds were needed and this provided a reason for more theatricals. The Amateur Company of the Guild of Literature and Art was formed and Dickens was unanimously chosen as general manager. Lytton wrote a five-act comedy, *Not so Bad as We Seem*, and Dickens and Mark Lemon wrote a farce, *Mr. Nightingale's Diary*. Dickens acted in both. In the comedy he played Lord Wilmot, a modish young gentleman, and in the farce he played the eccentric Mr. Gabblewig. In later revivals of the farce he sometimes played as many as five parts, changing his dress and his character with a rapidity which professional actors envied.

Dickens was the driving force behind these productions. He ruled the Company firmly, but without arrogance. He was punctual and methodical. Unlike most amateur companies, rehearsals were devoted to sheer hard work. All this resulted in a polished production. No detail was too small for him to overlook. On the day of the performance he was everywhere. He would even help the stage hands to erect the scenery, darting about in shirt sleeves, clutching a hammer and a bag of nails. Between 1851 and 1852 the Company performed in the provinces as well as in London. Dickens revelled in the life of a strolling player, especially so at this time, when it took him away from Catherine.

She was becoming even more clumsy. One evening at dinner in 1854, when they had guests, her bracelets slid off her arms and fell with a splash into her soup. At such times Dickens was all tenderness and solicitude. He tried to hide his irritation, but Catherine was always aware of it and this intensified her blundering. Since 1842 her younger sister, Georgina, had been living with them. Georgina Hogarth was very different from Catherine; she was bright, cheerful and efficient. The children adored her and turned to her rather than their mother. Over the years the running of the house had devolved more and more on Georgina and under her management everything went smoothly. By 1855 she was in absolute control of all domestic matters.

In the spring of 1856 Dickens was in a very depressed state. It was an agony for him to be in the same room with Catherine and he avoided her as much as he could. He was writing *Little Dorrit* and this was putting such a strain on his invention that he was forced to compile memoranda of suggestions for characters and incidents. He had never needed to do this in the past. His imagination had always teemed with characters. Some were still with him, but their ranks were pitifully thin. "The old days – the old days!" he wrote to Forster. "Shall I ever, I wonder, get the frame of mind back as it used to be then? Something of it perhaps – but never quite as it used to be."

Dickens had confided in John Forster since their friendship began in 1837, when they were both twenty-five years old. Even in those days Forster was sedate. He was a sturdily built, fresh-faced man, with a loud voice, an overbearing manner and a high opinion of himself. Dickens parodied him in *Our Mutual Friend* as Mr. Podsnap, "the Mr. Podsnap who was well-to-do and stood very high in Mr. Podsnap's opinion." Forster was a man of affairs with a passion for literature. Throughout their friendship he was possessive towards Dickens and he especially resented Wilkie Collins and Dickens's other bohemian friends. He wanted to be his only confidant. Dickens respected Forster's competence in business matters and discussed with him all the business side of authorship. Forster could advise him over contracts and publishers, but he could not ease the torments of a genius and in this crisis in Dickens's life he could do nothing to help him. The other cause of Dickens's misery, however, Forster could more easily comprehend. He had suspected for some time that all was not well between Dickens and his wife, and these suspicions were confirmed in the closing words of a letter he received from Dickens in April 1856: "I find that the skeleton in my domestic closet is becoming a pretty big one."

Throughout the summer of 1856 Dickens struggled on with *Little Dorrit*, but restlessness had become an habitual feeling with him and in the autumn he turned to rehearsing a melodrama by Wilkie Collins entitled *The Frozen Deep*. This play was inspired by the arctic expedition of Sir John Franklin, all the members of which had perished from exposure and starvation. Dickens was to play the part of Richard Wardour, an arctic explorer, who saves the life of his rival at the cost of his own by carrying him to safety over snow and ice to the feet of the girl they both love. Dickens was excited by the part and this sacrificial role became the outlet for his misery. He immersed himself in the part. He did not think his moustache and chin-tuft sufficient for an arctic explorer, so he began to grow a beard. He memorised his lines on long walks at night through Finchley and Willesden, shouting them out to the terror of passers-by.

The play was to be produced at Tavistock House on Twelfth Night of the following year and from October to January he rehearsed his company every Monday and Friday. After moving to Tavistock House in 1852, Dickens had converted the schoolroom into a miniature theatre, capable of holding an audience of ninety. On each Twelfth Night he and his children, together with his friends and their children, had staged a pantomime under his direction. The production for 1854 was Fielding's *Tom Thumb*, in which he played the Ghost of Gaffer Thumb. In 1855 he played the testy old Baron in Planché's *Fortunio and His Seven Gifted Servants*. In the summer of that year a more serious work was produced in the tiny theatre. This was *The Lighthouse*, a melodrama specially written by Wilkie Collins. Dickens played Aaron

Gurnock, a strange old lighthouse-keeper, who lived entirely in the past, and for the part his eyes assumed a sad lost look.

The Twelfth Night performance of *The Frozen Deep* was so successful that three repeat performances were given in January 1857. The intensity with which Dickens played the part of Richard Wardour was admired and talked about among his friends for weeks afterwards, but for Dickens the excitement ended with the final performance and he relapsed into his depressed state.

Nothing could give him pleasure, not even his new home at Gad's Hill. In February he took possession of the old house two miles outside Rochester, which from childhood he had dreamed of owning. At last his dream had come true, but it brought him no happiness. He craved for some activity to divert him. Then, in June, the death of Douglas Jerrold, the journalist, gave him the excuse for the excitement and distraction he sought. On the day of the funeral he called a meeting at the Garrick Club. He insisted that money must be raised for Jerrold's family and he proposed a series of entertainments. Thackeray would be asked to give a lecture. There would be a revival of *Black-Eyed Susan*, Jerrold's most successful play. He would give a Reading of the *Carol*, and *The Frozen Deep* would be performed.

While Dickens was genuinely concerned about the plight of Jerrold's family, he was chiefly motivated by his own need for distraction. Jerrold's son told him that the family were not in straitened circumstances and that he resented "the hat being carried round". But the preparations were already under way and Dickens gave them a momentum that nothing could stop. He flung himself into the organisation of the benefits. He set up an office at the Gallery of Illustration. In charge of all the business details, he placed Arthur Smith, brother and business manager of Albert Smith, the showman. He drove everyone. For two nights before the private performance of *The Frozen Deep* for the Queen and Prince Albert, he rehearsed his company until long after midnight.

At the three public performances of *The Frozen Deep* at the

Gallery of Illustration the audiences were deeply moved by Dickens's portrayal of Richard Wardour. At the beginning of the play his mood was vindictive, but by the end this had changed, through suffering, to penitence. Dickens seemed to have put the whole of his unhappiness and frustration into the part. During the last act, when he rushed off the stage in anguish, he tossed the other actors aside like a charging bull. His heart-rending death scene reduced to tears not only the audience but also his fellow players. In the same month of July he gave two Readings of the *Carol* at the St. Martin's Hall. After the first Reading, he told Macready: "The two thousand and odd people were like one and their enthusiasm was something awful."

As part of the Jerrold benefits he read the *Carol* at Manchester, in the Free Trade Hall, on 31 July. *The Frozen Deep* was also to be presented there on 21 and 22 August. In that immense auditorium, capable of holding three thousand people, professional actresses would be needed to make their voices heard and their gestures seen. Dickens had to find substitutes for his daughters and other female members of the cast. He approached Alfred Wigan, manager of the Olympic Theatre, who recommended Mrs. Ternan and her daughters Maria and Ellen. Dickens rehearsed them for three days before the Manchester performances. At the end of the play, as Richard Wardour, he died with his head on Maria's lap. He died so movingly that, professional actress though she was, Maria could not help her emotions overcoming her. On the first night the tears fell down from her eyes like rain and flowed over his upturned face so that he could hardly speak for them. He whispered to her, "My dear child, it will be over in two minutes. Pray compose yourself," but she could not restrain her tears. On the second night, before an audience of three thousand, he gave the finest performance of all. Wilkie Collins wrote: "The trite phrase is the true phrase to describe that magnificent piece of acting. He literally electrified the audience."

Dickens had given the leading female part in *The Frozen Deep* to Maria Ternan because of her greater acting experience, but he was very struck by her younger sister, Ellen. He thought her "most attractive and a sweet little thing". Ellen Ternan was eighteen years old. She was very pretty, slightly built, with fair hair and blue eyes. Dickens had first met her backstage at the Haymarket Theatre. He came across her crying bitterly because of the briefness of the costume she had to wear for the part of the Grecian youth, Hippomenes, in Talfourd's play *Atalanta*. She told him that she was in tears at having "to show so much leg" and he had been touched by her modesty. Although she had only a small part in *The Frozen Deep*, she played opposite him in *Uncle John*, the farce that followed. During rehearsals he found her captivating and by the end of the Manchester performances he was infatuated with her.

The benefit performances raised two thousand pounds. The Jerrold family had forgotten their resentment and were grateful and touched by this magnificent total. With the theatrical excitements over, Dickens was again depressed. Moreover, he was suffering from intense reaction. He felt hemmed in on all sides and he believed that he must break out or he would die. He proposed to Collins that they take a long trip together: "I want to escape from myself. For when I *do* start up and stare myself seedily in the face, as happens to be my case at present, my blankness is inconceivable – indescribable – my misery amazing." In early September they set off for a walking tour in Cumberland.

Before leaving he confessed to Forster: "Poor Catherine and I are not made for each other, and there is no help for it. It is not only that she makes me uneasy and unhappy, but that I make her so too – and much more so. She is exactly what you know, in the way of being amiable and complying; but we are strangely ill-assorted for the bond there is between us." The mere unburdening of himself to Forster was a relief in his present state and the cool mountain air of Cumberland helped to clear his mind. He realised that whatever the circumstances of their marriage both he and Catherine must come to terms with them. He believed that an immediate change in their domestic arrangements would help towards this end. Before his return to London he wrote to Anne Cornelius, his old servant at Tavistock House, instructing her to transform his dressing-room into his bedroom. The doorway between Catherine's bedroom and the dressing-room was to be closed by a wooden door and the recess filled with shelves. He told Anne that these changes were not to be talked about and that the sooner they were done the better. After twenty-one years of marriage, he no longer wanted to share the same bedroom with Catherine. For the sake of their children and the world he was willing to remain her husband, but only in appearance.

Neither this decision nor the trip to Cumberland diminished his restlessness. *Little Dorrit* was completed and he longed more than ever for some excuse, like the Jerrold benefits, to fling himself into a fury of activity. On his return from Cumberland, when Forster cautioned him, comparing his recent rush up Carrock Fell with his rush into other difficulties, Dickens replied: "Too late to say, put the curb on, and don't rush at hills – the wrong man to say it to. I have now no relief but in action. I am incapable of rest. I am quite confident I should rust, break, and die, if I spared myself. Much better to die, doing. What I am in that way, nature made me first, and my way of life has of late, alas! confirmed."
Later that autumn he believed he had found the activity he sought. Since the Birmingham Readings of December 1853, he had read the *Carol* two or three times a year for charity, but the requests he received were so numerous that as early as 1854 he had realised that he must either give up reading altogether or adopt it for his own profit. He was aware of the large sums of money the Readings made for the charities in which he happened to be interested and he knew that he had only to stretch out his hand to grasp a fortune. From Gad's Hill he wrote to Forster: "What do you think of my paying for this place by reviving that old idea of some readings from my books? I am strongly tempted. Think of it."
Forster was opposed to the idea. He told Dickens that a professional Reader had in it so much the character of a public

exhibition as to call into question his standing as a writer. It was true that other eminent writers, including Thackeray, had given lectures for their own profit, but this was like descending to the vulgarity of the stage. He even feared that it could lead to Dickens following his old ambition of becoming a professional actor. The fact that he himself had acted with Dickens for charitable causes he considered beside the point. So was the fact that their friend Macready and many other actors were men of the highest character. For a literary artist to become a professional showman was a lowering of dignity, it was a substitution of lower for higher aims.

Dickens did not agree. He told Forster that he saw no loss of dignity in reading from his own books. If charitable causes might legitimately profit from it, why should not he? Moreover, it would keep him busy, provide an outlet for his restlessness and take him away from a miserable situation at home. He also had reason to believe that he would make a lot of money and if this were so, then reading could provide an alternative livelihood should his literary talent ever fail him.

The question rested until the following spring, when Dickens put the matter to his friend Miss Coutts. She saw nothing derogatory in it. She thought that most people would be glad that he should have the money rather than anyone else. She told him that it might be misunderstood at first, but very soon everyone would appreciate what he was doing.

He consulted Albert Smith, the showman, who was one of the bohemian set with whom he now spent so much of his time. Smith was a well-known figure in literary and theatrical circles. He was a novelist, a dramatist and a journalist, and since 1850 he had made a great reputation as an entertainer. His one-man shows were a popular feature of the London scene. They were travelogues, illustrated by dioramic views and laced with comic songs and sketches. It was Smith who had started the fashion of writers appearing on the public platform. Thackeray had since set a higher standard, but Smith had scored the first success.

This growing fashion aroused the wrath of some literary men, who thought, like Forster, that the bringing in of the comic actor element – mimicking the voice and gesture to heighten the effect of the humorous passages – was beneath the dignity of the literary calling. In this respect, Thomas Carlyle commented, Thackeray's complete lack of acting ability told in his favour. Nor could they tolerate the Barnum-like publicity methods Smith used to attract attention to his entertainments. Dickens, on the other hand, shared with Smith a keen awareness of the value of publicity. When he was bringing out a new book, London was flooded with bright orange posters.

Smith not only encouraged Dickens to go ahead with the Readings but also suggested that his brother, Arthur Smith, who acted as his business manager, should act in the same capacity for Dickens. Dickens welcomed this offer. During the Jerrold benefits Arthur Smith had been in charge of all the business details and Dickens had been impressed by his efficiency. Moreover, he could now tell Forster that the whole enterprise would be conducted with dignity, because he himself would not touch the business side. But Forster remained immovable. He was pained that Dickens was seeking the advice of such a man as Albert Smith. In his opinion, public performances by hacks like Smith were all very well, but they should not become the chief activity of the greatest literary genius of the age. He was coming to believe, however, that Dickens had already made up his mind.

Dickens had not made up his mind, but his decision was hastened by two charity Readings he had promised to give of the *Carol*, one in Edinburgh on 26 March in aid of the Philosophical Institution and the other in London on 15 April in aid of the Hospital for Sick Children, Great Ormond Street. Before leaving for Edinburgh he told Forster that his arguments were irrational. Forster had raised no objection to his reading for charity, yet was not a public exhibition of himself taking place equally, no matter who got the money? Many people already supposed him to be paid. Every week he received about twenty letters asking him at

Charles Dickens giving a reading

Mrs. Charles Dickens

what price and on what terms he would read. "Why, at this very time, half Scotland believes that I am paid for going to Edinburgh. Here is Greenock writes to me, and asks could it be done for a hundred pounds? There is Aberdeen writes, and states the capacity of its hall, and says, though far less profitable than the very large hall in Edinburgh, is it not enough to come on for?"

He was becoming more and more convinced that reading would give him the distraction he sought. He told Collins: "The domestic unhappiness remains so strong upon me that I can't write, and (waking) can't rest, one minute. I have never known a moment's peace or content since the last night of *The Frozen Deep*. I do suppose that there never was a man so seized and rended by one spirit. In this condition, though nothing can alter or soften it, I have a turning notion that the mere physical effort and change of the Readings would be good, as another means of bearing it."

In Edinburgh he read to an audience of two thousand people. The experience was so stimulating that he made up his mind to read professionally. He explained his decision to Forster: "I must do *something*, or I shall wear my heart away. I can see no better thing to do that is half so hopeful in itself, or half so well suited to my restless state." Forster feared that the unsettled habits connected with reading could only make more difficult any chance of a better understanding with Catherine, but when he voiced these fears, Dickens replied: "Quite dismiss from your mind any reference whatever to present circumstances at home. Nothing can put *them* right, until we are all dead and buried and risen. It is not, with me, a matter of will, or trial, or sufferance, or good humour, or making the best of it, or making the worst of it, any longer. It is all despairingly over. Have no lingering hope of, or for, me in this association. A dismal failure has to be borne, and there is an end."

He begged Forster to consider the project apart from personal feelings and to advise him on how it would affect his relations with his public. This relationship was an affectionate one and he valued it highly. Throughout the charity Readings the audiences had shown their appreciation, but would they applaud him as much when they knew he was reading for his own profit? Would the Public Readings have any influence on the sales of his next book? If they had an influence at all, would it be a good or bad one? Forster could not answer these questions, nor could Arthur Smith, who told Dickens: "Of the immense return in money I have no doubt. Of the Dash into the new position, however, I am not so good a judge."

The early signs of public reaction to Dickens's new status were encouraging. His first professional appearance was to take place on 29 April at the St. Martin's Hall. Before that he was announced to read the *Carol* in the same place on 15 April in aid of the Hospital for Sick Children. The tickets for the charity Reading were quickly sold, with people coming every day for more. As all the seats had gone, they asked to be booked for one of the forthcoming professional Readings. No one complained that Dickens would be getting the money and not a charity.

On the evening of Thursday, 29 April, 1858, Charles Dickens made his first appearance on a platform as a professional Reader. The Reading selected for the occasion was *The Cricket on the Hearth*, but before commencing he addressed a few words to the immense audience. He told them that it had become impossible to comply with the accumulating demands for charity Readings and that he had had to choose between reading on his own account or not reading at all. He had had little or no difficulty in deciding on the former course. Three reasons had led him to make this decision. Firstly, he was satisfied that it involved no compromise of literature. Secondly, he believed that whatsoever brought a public man and his public face to face, in terms of mutual confidence and respect, was a good thing. Thirdly, he had had experience of the interest his hearers took in the Readings and of the delight they gave to him, as a tried means of strengthening those relations of personal friendship, which it was his great privilege and pride, as it was his great responsibility, to hold with a multitude of persons who would never hear his voice or see his face. "Thus it is," he added, with a smile, "that I come, quite naturally, to be here among you at this time. And thus it is that I proceed to read this little book, quite as composedly as I might proceed to write it, or to publish it in any other way."

And so Charles Dickens began his career as a professional reader and he did not close it until the spring of 1870, three months before his death.

The Start of the Race

2

DICKENS DOES IT CAPITALLY

THE PLATFORM arrangements for the Readings at the St. Martin's Hall could not have been simpler. In the centre stood a reading desk of novel and graceful design. The top was supported on four slender legs. On the left of the reader, screwed into the flat top, was an oblong block; on the right, a few inches below the top, was a narrow shelf for a water carafe, a tumbler and a handkerchief. At floor level a two-inch-high wooden rail connected the four legs. The whole desk, top, legs and rails, was covered in maroon velvet. In the background was a screen of maroon cloth, of a darker shade than the desk. Three feet in front of the desk and twelve feet above ran a horizontal row of gas jets, with tin reflectors, supported by two vertical pipes. Midway in both these pipes was a powerful jet with a glass chimney. Thus, when Dickens was standing at the desk he was framed in bright light against a dark background and all his gestures and expressions could be clearly seen by the audience.

Simple as these arrangements were, every detail had been carefully thought out by Dickens. He considered the gas lights to be so important that throughout his reading career he employed his own gas man. He had designed his reading desk with great skill. While holding the book, he could rest his elbow on the oblong block and still maintain an upright position. While standing behind the desk, almost all his body could be seen by the audience and this was essential to the effect of the Readings. He had realised the need for a specially designed desk after one of the charity Readings, when he had been hampered by the desk provided for him, which had been so high and enclosed that only his head and shoulders could be seen. His own desk was to become an integral part of the Readings. By slamming it violently with the palm of his hand, he conjured up the ferocious Squeers bringing his school to order; by drumming on it with his fingertips, he brought out all the gaiety of the Fezziwigs' ball.

These platform arrangements were in striking contrast to the theatres of the day, with their gorgeous costumes and magnificent scenic illusions. Yet it was their very simplicity which gave the maximum stage effect to the Readings. With so few aids, Dickens peopled the platform with a host of characters.

Between 29 April and 22 July, 1858, he gave seventeen Readings at the St. Martin's Hall. Every performance was crowded and the waiting carriages stretched down Long Acre to Leicester Square. The announcement of the Readings had, of course, aroused great interest. Dickens was the most popular author in the English-speaking world. The names and sayings of his characters were already part of the language. His books had sounded a response in the hearts of his readers and through them countless people had come to love him. No other writer had ever enjoyed such a relationship with his readers. The Readings appealed, as did the books, to all ages and to all tastes, cultivated and simple. At Thackeray's lectures or at Albert Smith's entertainments the audiences were predominantly middle-class, but at the Readings all classes were represented from the aristocrat in the five-shilling stall to the working man in the shilling gallery. It was this universal appeal that put the Readings in a different category from all other entertainments.

Precisely at eight o'clock Dickens came on to the platform, book in hand, and took his place at the reading desk. He was in evening dress with a red flower in his buttonhole. He acknowledged with a smile the tremendous applause which greeted him. Some of the audience were there simply to gaze at the writer whom they had come to think of as a much-loved, but unknown friend. They saw a man forty-six years old, a little above average in height, with a slender figure and an alert carriage. The head was nobly shaped and crowned with long brown hair, which had receded above the temples. The face was handsome and animated, long and thin, with shaved cheeks, moustache and pointed beard. The eyes were the most remarkable feature, dark brown and of extraordinary brilliance.

Dickens stood there, patiently and cheerfully, waiting for everything to be quiet in the packed hall, then he opened the book and began to read. His voice was deep and exquisitely modulated. One slight fault was a hissing sound in pronouncing the letter "s". With his voice his expressive hands came into play and for emphasis he held a paper knife. Early on in his reading career Dickens realised that he must free his eyes from the book, because it was impossible for him to achieve the greatest dramatic impact when his eyes were downcast. He therefore set about learning his texts by heart and eventually he held the book merely for effect.

In one of the Readings in this first London season it was essential for his eyes to be seen by the audience. This was in *The Poor Traveller*, a short Reading adapted from a story published in *Household Words*. The hero of this Reading, set in the times of the Napoleonic Wars, was Dick Doubledick, a wild young man, who, having made a mess of his life, enlisted in the army in the hope of getting killed. But he did not take kindly to army discipline and was constantly being punished. "Now the captain of Doubledick's company," Dickens told his audience, "was a young gentleman not above five years his senior, whose eyes had an expression in them which affected Private Doubledick in a very remarkable way." Doubledick could never meet those eyes without a sense of shame and he was dismayed when, after forty-eight hours in the cells, he was summoned to the captain's quarters. "Private Doubledick pulled off his cap," said Dickens, "took a stride forward and stood in the light of the dark bright eyes." At this point in the Reading, out of Dickens's own eyes would look the eyes of the captain as he had described them, "bright, handsome dark eyes, what are called laughing eyes generally, and when serious rather steady than severe." In the repertoire of the Readings, Dickens's eyes were to express many moods, ranging from demonic fury to tender pity.

The Cricket on the Hearth was the first Reading to be given at the St. Martin's Hall, followed on subsequent nights by *The Chimes* and the *Carol*. *The Cricket* and *The Chimes*, like their companion Christmas story the *Carol*, were wonderful mixtures of humour, pathos and terror. Both, too, had their share of mean-spirited characters. In *The Cricket* there was Tackleton, the malicious toy merchant, who "had been living on children all his life, and was their implacable enemy". In *The Chimes* there were Alderman Cute and Mr. Filer, who sowed the seeds of their own discontent in the little porter, Trotty Veck.

When the audience first met Trotty he was happy enough. His pretty daughter, Meg, had just brought him his lunch in a covered basket and he was sniffing in an attempt to guess its contents. The scene was played by Dickens with a mouth-watering relish: "It ain't – I suppose it ain't polonies? No. It's – it's mellower than polonies. It's too decided for trotters. Liver? No! There's a mildness about it that don't answer to liver. Pettitoes? No. It ain't faint enough for pettitoes. It wants the stringiness of cock's heads. And I know it ain't sausage. I'll tell you what it is. No, it isn't neither. Why, what am I thinking of! I shall forget my own name next. It's tripe!"

Trotty was played by Dickens in a voice modified from Bob

Cratchit's in the *Carol* and, as in the case of the timid ill-paid clerk, the idea of physical weakness and simple goodness came over perfectly. Trotty's plaintive chant of "Here we are and here we go" as he ran homewards carrying the half-starved child, Lilian, in his arms, produced both tears and laughter in the audience.

As with *The Cricket* and the *Carol*, the moods of *The Chimes* changed quickly, from Trotty's discontent to his terror, when he was called by the Bells and climbed up the church tower. There he saw "dwarf phantoms, spirits, elfin creatures of the Bells. He saw them leaping, flying, dropping, pouring from the Bells without a pause." The Goblin of the Great Bell called him to account and showed him how the seeds of discontent would grow not only in himself but also in those he loved. Scenes of the future were brought before his eyes, the most terrible being the suicide of his daughter.

The Chimes ended with Trotty awaking from his dream, beside himself with joy to find that all the shame and despair he had witnessed were gone and to hear the Bells ringing in the New Year.

In the middle of June *The Story of Little Dombey* was added to the repertoire and also a triple bill comprised of three short Readings, *The Poor Traveller*, *Boots at the Holly Tree Inn* and *Mrs. Gamp*. For the autumn tour Dickens was to add two short comic pieces adapted from *Pickwick Papers*. These were *The Trial from Pickwick* and *Mr. Bob Sawyer's Party* and were used to follow one of the longer Readings in the manner of the theatrical convention of the farce following the melodrama and for the same reason, to send the audience home in a light-hearted mood.

The texts which Dickens adapted as Readings were those that gave him the greatest chance to impersonate a wide range of characters. The Readings did not give him many opportunities for playing a sustained role, but they did afford him far more scope than the amateur theatricals had done to use his countless voices and faces. In adapting the books as Readings it was the actor, or rather the impersonator, in Dickens which came first, not the writer. He did not, therefore, regard the texts as sacrosanct. Two separate sections of *Martin Chuzzlewit* were brought together to make the *Mrs. Gamp* Reading. He pruned his texts ruthlessly to achieve the maximum dramatic effects. In the original account of the *Carol* the description of Mr. Fezziwig's dancing ends with the words: "Fezziwig 'cut' – cut so deftly, that he appeared to wink with his legs and came upon his feet again without a stagger." In the Reading Dickens left out the words that come after "legs", saying, with a spasmodic shake of the head and a twist of the paper knife, "He cut – cut so deftly, that he appeared to – wink with his legs."

Descriptions of characters were eliminated when he could convey their appearance by acting. As his audiences were already familiar with the characters, he had no need to hold back the action by explaining who they were. He interpolated new matter wherever he thought fit. Mr. Justice Stareleigh and Bob Sawyer were both given words to say in the Reading that do not appear in the book.

These revisions continued as he rehearsed the Readings, sometimes as often as two hundred times. Even when he read them publicly, he did not regard the texts as final. He revised them again and again in the light of audience reaction. The pages of his prompt copies show lines and sometimes entire passages obliterated in washes of black, blue or red ink. The margins are filled with balloons of writing and cobwebs of lines indicating interpolations and corrections. They also contain directions jotted down for his own guidance such as, "Snap your fingers", "Rising action", "Soften very much", "Cheerful", "Tone to mystery", and many others.

Dickens never considered the Readings a by-product of his writing. As with everything he undertook he gave them all his care and thought. Throughout his reading career he strived constantly to improve them. Ten years after his first season at the St. Martin's Hall he was to tell his son, Charley, that he had never read to an audience without watching "for an opportunity of striking out something better somewhere". The long success of the Readings could not have been possible without this high professional standard.

Over the years Dickens was to add other Readings to his repertoire, but some of those in the first series were to remain unsurpassed. The *Carol* was the greatest favourite of all. *Little Dombey* was the most pathetic. *Boots* was the happiest and the *Pickwick Trial* was the funniest, closely followed by *Mrs. Gamp*. Mr. Justice Stareleigh in the *Pickwick Trial* was Dickens's greatest comic performance as a reader. R. C. Lehmann has recorded his amazement, when it seemed that Dickens had vanished from the platform and in his place had come "a fat, pompous, pursy little man, with a plump, imbecile face, from which every vestige of good temper and cheerfulness had been removed. The upper lip had become long, the corners of the mouth drooped, the nose was short and podgy, all the angles of the chin had gone, the chin itself had receded into the throat, and the eyes, lately so humorous and human, had become as malicious and obstinate as those of a pig."

The malice and obstinacy of the little judge were best seen when he browbeat the flustered Mr. Winkle, who had just taken the witness stand to be examined by Mr. Skimpin, junior counsel for the plaintiff.

> "Now, sir, have the goodness to let his Lordship and the jury know what your name is, will you?" Mr. Skimpin inclined his head on one side, and listened with the greatest sharpness for the answer, as if to imply that he rather thought Mr. Winkle's natural taste for perjury would induce him to give some name which did not belong to him.
> "Winkle".
> *Court*. "Have you any Christian name, sir?"
> "Nathaniel, sir."
> *Court*. "Daniel, – any other name?"

"Nathaniel, sir, – my Lord, I mean."

Court. "Nathaniel Daniel or Daniel Nathaniel?"

"No, my Lord, only Nathaniel; not Daniel at all."

Court. "What did you tell me it was Daniel for, then, sir?"

"I didn't, my Lord."

Court. "You did, sir. How could I have got Daniel on my notes, unless you told me so, sir?"

Another moment of glorious farce was the little judge's intervention earlier in the Reading, when Sergeant Buzfuz for the plaintiff was examining Mrs. Elizabeth Cluppins as to how she happened to be in Mrs. Bardell's back room at the time of Mr. Pickwick's alleged proposal of marriage.

Court. "What were you doing in the back room, ma'am?"

"My Lord and jury, I will not deceive you."

Court. "You had better not, ma'am."

"I was there unbeknown to Mrs. Bardell. I had been out with a little basket, gentlemen, to buy three pounds of red kidney purtaties, which was three pound tuppence ha'penny, when I see Mrs. Bardell's street door on the jar."

Court. "On the what?"

"Partly open, my Lord."

Court. "She *said* on the jar."

"It's all the same, my Lord."

The little judge looked doubtful, and said he'd make a note of it.

Dickens again achieved complete identification with the character when he played Cobbs, the Boots, in *Boots at the Holly Tree Inn*, a Reading adapted from his Christmas story *The Holly Tree*. The embodiment of Cobbs stood before the audience, his eyes half-closed, his body swaying to and fro, his voice sounding as if he were chewing a straw. "What was the curiousest thing he had ever seen? Well? He didn't know. He couldn't momently name what was the curiousest thing he had seen, – unless it was a

Unicorn, – and he see *him* once at a Fair. But supposing a young gentleman not eight year old was to run away with a fine young woman of seven, might I think *that* a queer start? Certainly! Then that was a start as he himself had had his blessed eyes on, – and he had cleaned the shoes they run away in, – and they was so little that he couldn't get his hand into 'em."

Then Cobbs proceeded to tell in his own naïve way the story of Master Harry Walmers, Junior, who fell in love with his cousin, Norah, and started with her for Gretna Green to be married. "It was a very happy notion," John Hollingshead remarked, "to place such a pretty story in the mouth of such a man; and the audience, while they watch with interest the progress of the fanciful episode in the life of the little runaway children, are amused by the broad humour and strong individuality of the simulated narrator."

On their way to Gretna Green the two children stopped at the Holly Tree Inn, where they were recognised by Cobbs, who had formerly been in the service of the little boy's father. Cobbs described their arrival at the inn and repeated their dinner order, "Mutton chops and cherry pudding for two." He also enumerated their articles of luggage, the lady having "a parasol, a smelling-bottle, a round and a half of cold buttered toast, eight peppermint drops, and a doll's hairbrush. The gentleman had got about a dozen yards of string, a knife, three or four sheets of writing-paper folded up surprisingly small, an orange and a Chaney mug with his name on it." The children confided their intention in Cobbs. He told the landlord, who immediately set off to inform the relatives.

Cobbs was remorseful that he was the one who had betrayed the children and he wished with all his heart that "there was any impossible place, where those two babies could make an impossible marriage and live impossibly happy ever afterwards". When the boy's father arrived, Cobbs conducted him upstairs and at the door of the room he paused and said, "I beg your pardon, sir. I hope you are not angry with Master Harry. For Master Harry's a fine boy and will do you credit and honour."

Cobbs's appreciation of Master Harry Walmer, Junior, was shared by all the female servants at the inn. "The way in which the women of that house – *without* exception – *every* one of 'em – married *and* single – took to that boy when they heard the story, is surprising. It was as much as could be done to keep 'em from dashing into the room and kissing him. They climbed up all sorts of places, at the risk of their lives, to look at him through a pane of glass. *And they were seven deep at the keyhole!*"

These ladies were even more excited when the boy asked his father if he might kiss Norah before he went home. The father took his hand and Cobbs led the way to the bedroom where the little girl lay fast asleep in an enormous bed. As the father lifted the boy up to kiss her sleeping face, one of the chambermaids, who was peeping through the door, called out – and here Dickens put on the shrillest of voices – "*It's a shame to part 'em!*"

Kate Field observed that this particular chambermaid seemed to spring from Dickens's head "as Minerva sprang from the head of Jove," armed and ready for the fray. It was one of the most remarkable things about the Readings that characters of little importance in the books emerged on the platform as well-defined individuals, living and breathing. There were the business men in the *Carol* who discourse upon Scrooge's death:

"No," said a great fat man with a monstrous chin. "I don't know much about it either way. I only know he's dead."

"When did he die?" inquired another.

"Last night, I believe."

"Why, what was the matter with him? I thought he'd never die."

"God knows," said the first, with a yawn.

"What has he done with his money?" asked a red-faced gentleman.

"I haven't heard," said the man with the large chin. "Company, perhaps. He hasn't left it to me. That's all I know. Bye, bye."

Only a dozen lines are devoted to this episode, yet in the Reading each man stood forth clearly, especially the great fat man with the monstrous chin.

The brief conversation between the Tugbys, often passed over by most readers of *The Chimes*, provided some of the biggest laughs in the Reading. Mr. and Mrs. Tugby were fat and rosy-cheeked. "They were but two," Dickens told his audience, "but they were red enough for ten." Tugby's voice, as spoken by Dickens and described in the book, was "a fat whisper". When the audience met them the Tugbys had just finished their tea. Tugby was sitting comfortably by the fire, while Mrs. Tugby reported to him on the state of the weather outside. "Blowing and sleeting hard and threatening snow," she told him. "Dark. And very cold." "I'm glad to think we had muffins," said Mr. Tugby. "It's a sort of night that's meant for muffins. Likewise crumpets. Also Sally Lunns."

Not even Trotty Veck with his basin of tripe nor the Cratchit family with their Christmas dinner could scale the epicurean heights achieved by Mr. Tugby in the savouring of his muffins. The geniality and relish which Dickens as a reader brought to these descriptions of food caused Charles Kent to apply to him the compliment bestowed by Charles Lamb on the comic actor, Joseph Munden, that "he understood a leg of mutton in its quiddity".

Again and again in the Readings Dickens lighted up neglected corners of his works. Mrs. Raddle's housemaid, Betsey, is often unnoticed in *Pickwick Papers*; she has, indeed, very little to say. In *Mr. Bob Sawyer's Party*, however, from the moment she opened her mouth to say, "Please Mr. Sawyer, Mrs. Raddle wants to speak to *you*," her dull level voice ending on the last mono-syllable in a wonderful series of inflections, she emerged as an incomparably comic character.

The use of inflection, especially rising inflection, in the enun-ciation of syllables was one of Dickens's techniques for achieving a comic effect. In *Little Dombey*, when Mrs. Blimber remarked that "if she could have known Cicero, she thought she could have died contented", he went up and down several octaves on the name *Cicero*. He used the same technique throughout Sergeant Buzfuz's opening address for the plaintiff in the *Pickwick Trial*. Sergeant Buzfuz began by saying that "never in the whole course of his professional experience – never, from the very first moment of applying himself to the study and practice of the *law*, had he approached a case with such a heavy sense of *re-spon-si-bi-li-ty* imposed upon him, – a *re-spon-si-bi-li-ty* he could never have *su-pport-ed* were he not buoyed up and *sus-tained* by a conviction so strong that it amounted to positive *cer-tain-ty*, that the cause of truth and justice, or, in other words, the cause of his much-injured and most oppressed client must *pre-vail . . .*" The actions accompanying the words "must prevail" were equally comic in their effect. To add impressiveness to them, a muscular contortion starting in the back of Dickens's neck rippled up and down his shoulders, as he drew back his head, thrust it forward and brought down his fist with a mighty slam on the reading desk.

In his interpretations of Sergeant Buzfuz, Mr. Justice Stareleigh, Scrooge, Cobbs and Bob Cratchit, Dickens achieved complete identification with the characters, but he was not always so successful. Paradoxically, his interpretations of characters so typically Dickensian as Sam Weller and Mr. Pecksniff were considered to be failures. Perhaps these characters were so much larger than life, so "like Gods", as Chesterton described them, that not even their creator could impersonate them without falling short of the conception people had formed of them. But if Mr. Pecksniff was a failure in *Mrs. Gamp*, the eponymous heroine herself was a triumph. As Mrs. Gamp, Dickens gave a comic performance of the highest order.

The Reading began with Mr. Pecksniff setting out in a hackney-cab to arrange for the funeral of old Anthony Chuzzlewit. He arrived, in due course, in Kingsgate Street, High Holborn, in search of Mrs. Gamp, "a nurse and watcher, and performer of nameless offices about the persons of the dead". His performance on the knocker of her door aroused the whole neighbourhood, the knocker being so ingeniously constructed "as to wake the street with ease, without making the smallest impression on the premises to which it was addressed". When "every window in the street became alive with female heads", Dickens's eyes distended at the extraordinary spectacle.

Everyone aroused was under the impression that Mr. Pecksniff was "upon an errand touching not the close of life, but the other end". He was urged on, especially by the married ladies. "Knock at the winder, sir, knock at the winder! Lord bless you, don't lose no more time than you can help – knock at the winder!" Mrs. Gamp, when aroused, was under the same misapprehension. When Mr. Pecksniff explained the object of his visit, Mrs. Gamp, who had a face for all occasions, immediately put on her mourning countenance, but the surrounding ladies berated her visitor, asking him what he meant by terrifying delicate females "with his corpses!" Mr. Pecksniff drove off with Mrs. Gamp "overwhelmed with popular execration".

In the cab Mrs. Gamp conversed with Mr. Pecksniff. To bring out her character Dickens made repeated asides to the audience. " 'And so the gentleman's dead, sir! Ah! The more's the pity,' – she didn't even know his name – 'But it's what we must all come to. It's as certain as being born, except that we can't make our calculations as exact. Ah! Poor dear!' "

"She was a fat old woman, this Mrs. Gamp," Dickens told his audience, "with a husky voice and a moist eye. Having very little neck, it cost her some trouble to look over herself, if one may say so, at those to whom she talked. She wore a rusty black gown, rather the worse for [snuff, and a shawl and bonnet to correspond. The face of Mrs. Gamp – the nose in particular – was somewhat red and swollen, and it was difficult to enjoy her society without becoming conscious of a smell of spirits."

Miss Ellen Ternan

Miss Georgina Hogarth (from a painting by Augustus Egg R.A.)

" 'Ah!' repeated Mrs. Gamp – for that was always a safe sentiment in cases of mourning – 'ah, dear! When Gamp was summonsed to his long home, and I see him a-lying in the hospital with a penny-piece on each eye, and his wooden leg under his left arm, I thought I should have fainted away. But I bore up.' "

If certain whispers current in the Kingsgate Street circles had any truth in them, Mrs. Gamp had indeed borne up surprisingly, and had exerted such uncommon fortitude as to dispose of Mr. Gamp's remains for the benefit of science.

"You have become indifferent since then, I suppose?" said Mr. Pecksniff. "Use is second nature, Mrs. Gamp."

"You may well say second nature, sir. One's first ways is to find sich things a trial to the feelings, and such is one's lasting custom. If it wasn't for the nerve a little sip of liquor gives me (which I was never able to do more than taste it), I never could go through with what I sometimes has to do. 'Mrs. Harris,' I says, at the wery last case I ever acted in, which it was but a young person, – 'Mrs. Harris,' I says, 'leave the bottle on the chimley-piece, and don't ask me to take none, but let me put my lips to it when I am so dispoged, and then I will do what I am engaged to do, according to the best of my ability.' 'Mrs. Gamp,' she says, in answer, 'if ever there was a sober creetur to be got at eighteenpence a day for working people, and three and six for gentlefolks, – night watching being a extra charge – you are that inwallable person.' 'Mrs. Harris,' I says to her, 'don't name the charge, for if I could afford to lay all my fellow-creeturs out for nothink, I would gladly do it, sich is the love I bears 'em.' "

"At this point, she was fain to stop for breath," Dickens said confidentially. "And advantage may be taken of the circumstance, to state that a fearful mystery surrounded this lady of the name of Harris, whom no one in the circle of Mrs. Gamp's acquaintance had ever seen; neither did any human being know her place of residence. There were conflicting rumours on the subject; but the prevalent opinion was that she was a phantom of Mrs. Gamp's brain, created for the purpose of holding complimentary dialogues with her on all manner of subjects."

The next character to be introduced was Mr. Mould, the undertaker. He had a face in which "a queer attempt at melancholy was at odds with a smirk of satisfaction". Speaking of old Chuzzlewit's funeral, which had been ordered by his son "with no limitation, positively no limitation in point of expense", Mr. Mould observed to Mr. Pecksniff: "This is one of the most impressive cases, sir, that I have seen in the whole course of my professional experience. Anything so filial as this – anything so honourable to human nature, anything *so* expensive, anything so calculated to reconcile all of us to the world we live in – never yet came under my observation. It only proves, sir, what was so forcibly expressed by the lamented poet, – buried at Stratford, – that there is good in everything."

The manner of Mr. Mould's departure as described in the Reading was acted out on the platform by Dickens: "Mr. Mould was going away with a brisk smile, when he remembered the occasion. Quickly becoming depressed again, he sighed; looked into the crown of his hat, as if for comfort; put it on without finding any; and slowly departed."

There followed an intimate description of Mrs. Gamp entering on her official duties for the night.

Firstly, she put on a yellow-white nightcap of prodigious size, in shape resembling a cabbage, having previously divested herself of a row of bald old curls, which could scarcely be called false, they were so innocent of anything approaching to deception; secondly and lastly, she summoned the housemaid, to whom she delivered this official charge, in tones expressive of faintness:

"I think, young woman, as I could peck a little bit o' pickled salmon, with a little sprig o' fennel, and a little sprinkling o' white pepper. I takes new bread, my dear, with just a pat o' fredge butter and a mossel o' cheese. With respects to ale, if they draws the Brighton old tipper at any 'ouse nigh here, I takes that all at night, my love; not as I cares for it myself, but on accounts of its being considered wakeful by the doctors; and whatever you do, young woman, don't bring me more than a shilling's worth of gin-and-water, warm, when I rings the bell a second time; for that is always my allowange, and I never takes a drop beyond. In case there should be sich a thing as a cowcumber in the 'ouse, I'm rather partial to 'em, though I am but a poor woman. Rich folks may ride on camels, but it ain't so easy for them to see out of a needle's eye. That is my comfort, and I hopes I knows it."

The Reading ended with Mrs. Gamp awaking at the close of her night watch and being relieved by Mrs. Betsey Prig. Mrs. Prig was also a nurse and a bosom-friend of Mrs. Gamp. She was of the Gamp build, but not so fat; her voice was deeper and more like a man's. She also had a beard. These two ladies often used to "nuss together, turn about, one off, one on". The audience were told that Mrs. Prig relieved punctually that morning, but that she relieved in an ill-temper.

"The best of us have their failings," Dickens observed gravely, "and it must be conceded of Mrs. Prig, that if there were a blemish in the goodness of her disposition, it was a habit she had of not bestowing all its sharp and acid properties upon her patients (as a thoroughly amiable woman would have done), but of keeping a considerable remainder for the service of her friends."

She looked offensively at Mrs. Gamp, and winked her eye. Mrs. Gamp felt it necessary that Mrs. Prig should know her place, and be made sensible of her exact station in society. So she began a remonstrance with:

"Mrs. Harris, Betsey –"

"Bother Mrs. Harris!"

Mrs. Gamp looked at Betsey in amazement, incredulity, and indignation. Mrs. Prig, winking her eye tighter, folded her arms and uttered these tremendous words:

"I don't believe there's no sich a person!"

With these expressions, she snapped her fingers once, twice, thrice, each time nearer to the face of Mrs. Gamp, and then turned away as one who felt that there was now a gulf between them which nothing could ever bridge across.

So ended one of the funniest of the Readings.

Dickens's greatest talent as an actor was his astonishing power of evoking the humorous and the pathetic. He made his audiences laugh at Mrs. Gamp and he made them cry for little Paul Dombey.

The Story of Little Dombey, adapted from the early chapters of *Dombey and Son*, was the saddest of all the Readings, but it also contained some riotously funny sequences. Paul Dombey was Mr. Dombey's son and heir. His mother had died giving him birth and he himself was only a weakling. He caught every childish disease and he was crushed by them one after the other. He was an odd little boy, with something wan and wistful in his small face, and many were those who shook their heads significantly and said he was too old-fashioned. When Paul was nearly five years old, his father, who was uneasy about him, sent him to stay at Mrs. Pipchin's "select infantine boarding-house" at Brighton. But Paul grew more old-fashioned there without growing any stronger. His father, anxious for him to be brought forward rapidly, enrolled him as a student at Doctor Blimber's Academy, which was conducted on the hothouse or forcing principle. "All the boys blew before their time. Mental green-peas were produced at Christmas, and intellectual asparagus all the year round." Paul's health continued to fail, however, and he was brought home to die. The Reading had a special poignancy in an age when so many families had suffered the loss of a child.

In the early part of the Reading the humorous characters predominated. There was Mrs. Pipchin, a grim old lady, "with a mottled face like bad marble", who had acquired an immense reputation as "a great manager of children", and the secret of whose management was "to give them everything they didn't like and nothing that they did". There were two other small boarders in her house. These were Master Bitherstone, from India, and a certain Miss Pankey.

"As to Master Bitherstone," Dickens told his audience, "he objected so much to the Pipchinian system, that before Little Dombey had been established in the house five minutes he privately asked that young gentleman if he could give him any idea of the way back to Bengal. As to Miss Pankey, *she* was disabled from offering any remark by being in solitary confinement for the offence of having sniffed three times in the presence of visitors."

Little Dombey grew no stronger at Mrs. Pipchin's. He spent most of his days sitting in a little armchair by the fire and Mrs. Pipchin remarked that he was an old, old-fashioned child.

His sister, Florence, used to take him in a wheel-chair down to the margin of the sea. With the wind blowing on his face and the water coming up among the wheels of his chair, he wanted nothing more. He would often look eagerly at the horizon and once he asked Florence what place was over there. "She told him there was another country opposite, but he said he didn't mean that: he meant farther away – farther away! Very often afterwards, in the midst of their talk, he would break off, to try to understand what it was that the waves were always saying; and would rise up in his couch to look towards that invisible region, far away." The words "far away" as spoken by Dickens, sounded like a death-knell.

Dickens now introduced his audience to the learned Doctor Blimber and his household. The Doctor himself was a portly gentleman, with a highly polished bald head and a chin "so very double, that it was a wonder how he ever managed to shave into the creases". His wife was not so learned, but "she pretended to be and did that quite as well". His daughter "was dry and sandy with working in the graves of deceased languages. None of your live languages for Miss Blimber. They must be dead – stone dead – and then Miss Blimber dug them up like a Ghoul." His butler gave "quite a winey flavour to the table-beer", he poured it out so superbly.

In Doctor Blimber's Academy the favourite character with the audience was Toots, the head boy, or rather the "head and shoulder boy", for he was so much taller than the rest. In that intellectual forcing house, where all the boys blew before their time, Toots had "suddenly left off blowing one day, and remained in the establishment a mere stalk". People said the Doctor "had rather overdone it with young Toots, and that when he began to have whiskers, he left off having brains". He was now allowed to pursue his own course of study and he occupied his time chiefly in writing long letters to himself from persons of distinction.

From the moment Dickens first spoke as Toots, in tones so deep and in a manner so sheepish that "if a lamb had roared it couldn't have been more surprising", the audience took this character to their hearts. Throughout the remainder of the Reading, every time he opened his mouth to speak as Toots there was a burst of laughter even before he had uttered a word.

Among this humorous company the voice of Little Dombey was heard from time to time like a sad refrain. They were all fond of the odd little boy, especially Toots, and they all agreed that he was old-fashioned. At Doctor Blimber's his health continued to fail and in mid-summer he was taken home to die.

The great pathetic climax of the Reading was the death of Little Dombey. From beginning to end this was related by Dickens in a low voice except for one startling moment. This occurred at the beginning of the final scene when Little Dombey, troubled as he sometimes was by the thought of a swift-moving river, felt forced "to try to stop it; to stem it with his childish hands, or choke its way with sand; and when he saw it coming on, resistless, HE CRIED OUT!" The frightened cry of the dying child still sounded among the rafters of the St. Martin's Hall as Dickens added in a low voice, "But a word from Florence, who was always at his side, restored him to himself."

The end was near. The child had been laid down again, with his arms clasped about his sister's neck. The sun streamed in through the rustling blind and quivered on the opposite wall "like golden water". "He put his hands together, as he had been used to do at his prayers. He did not remove his arms to do it; but they saw him fold them so, behind his sister's neck.

" 'Mamma is like you, Floy. I know her by the face! But tell them that the print upon the stairs at school is not Divine enough. The light about the head is shining on me as I go.' "

The audience were weeping. Dickens, the matchless chronicler of the innocent and the defenceless, of the little workhouse boy and the little crippled boy, was standing by the death-bed of the little old-fashioned boy.

"The old, old fashion! The fashion that came in with our first parents, and will last unchanged until our race has run its course, and the wide firmament is rolled up like a scroll. The old, old fashion – Death!"

Dickens himself was weeping and he finished the Reading in a broken voice. "Oh, thank GOD, all who see it for that older fashion yet of Immortality. And look upon us, Angels of young children, with regards not quite estranged, when the swift river bears us to the ocean!"

All eyewitness accounts confirm Dickens's genius as a reader of his own works. The two books on the subject, one British by Charles Kent and one American by Kate Field, are complimentary to the point of adulation. According to newspaper reports the audiences were hysterical in their appreciation. Dickens was, of course, a great actor, but it is to be wondered how much the success of the Readings owed to his theatrical art and how much to the audiences themselves. It must be remembered that they knew the books as well as he did. They would begin to smile in anticipation of a comic phrase and Dickens, observing this, would sometimes pause before speaking the words which he knew would be greeted with shouts of laughter.

When Dickens impersonated Mrs. Gamp or Sergeant Buzfuz, the total effect did not come entirely from him. Images of these characters were already in the minds of the audience, not only verbal images through the descriptions in the books but also visual images through the illustrations. This was especially true of the illustrations of Phiz (Hablôt Knight Browne), who had illustrated so many of Dickens's books. Dickens and Phiz had always collaborated closely over the illustrations. Dickens knew precisely how he wanted his characters to look and Phiz reproduced these ideas perfectly. The characters as impersonated by Dickens must have borne a strong resemblance to the characters as depicted by Phiz and the clear sharp lines of these illustrations were already etched into the minds of the audience.

Dickens was certainly dependent on his audience for stimulus. Given a dull audience, a Reading, especially a long Reading, could sometimes flag. Given an appreciative audience, he could not only give a magnificent performance but could also, in a comic Reading such as the *Pickwick Trial*, indulge in ad-libs and impromptu gags.

The Readings were emotional occasions. Dickens was the best-loved author of the day and the audience showed their love for him every time he appeared on the platform. He, for his part, had always identified himself with the people. The Readings of the *Carol* and *Little Dombey* had overtones of a mystical union between himself and his audience. At the second charity Reading of the *Carol* at Birmingham the audience had animated him "to that extent that I felt as if we were all bodily going up into the clouds together". Throughout his reading career he was sometimes so much at one with his audience "as to be powerless to do other than laugh when they laughed and cry when they cried".

All else apart, it was a tremendous theatrical achievement to people a bare platform with a whole world of characters and to evoke such a wide range of moods. The Readings proved that Dickens was one of the greatest actors of his day, that he was, in the words of Thomas Carlyle, "a whole tragic comic heroic theatre visible, performing under one hat".

PART TWO

The Reading Tours 1858–67

Blazes of Triumph!
CHARLES DICKENS to W. H. WILLS
on the progress of the Readings

3

THIS AUTUMN OF ALL OTHERS

THE PUBLIC Readings at the St. Martin's Hall had barely
begun than Dickens's smouldering domestic troubles suddenly
exploded. A bracelet he had bought for Ellen Ternan was
delivered by mistake to his wife. When Catherine challenged
him over this, he claimed that the bracelet was an innocent gift.
Catherine did not believe him. She had met Ellen Ternan and
suspected the relationship between her husband and the girl to be
dangerous and serious. Dickens was enraged by Catherine's

suspicions. He could not bear his wife and older daughters to think that he had a mistress. He demanded that Catherine call on Ellen to prove that she harboured no bad thoughts against her. Catherine pleaded with him not to humiliate her in such a manner, but he was adamant. Katey, aged nineteen, and fully aware of the situation, was passing her mother's bedroom when she heard sobs. On entering she saw Catherine putting on a bonnet. "Your father has asked me to go and see Ellen Ternan," Catherine said. "You shall not go," said Katey; but Catherine went.

Dickens had again browbeaten his wife into doing his will, but the matter was not to rest there. At the beginning of May Catherine told her parents about Ellen Ternan. Mr. and Mrs. Hogarth had watched with concern the deterioration of their daughter's marriage. Mrs. Hogarth, especially, blamed Dickens and resented him. On the advice of her parents, Catherine decided to leave Dickens and demand a separate maintenance. This solid family front was split, however, when their other daughter, Georgina, took Dickens's side. No one knew better than she the deep unhappiness of the marriage and she believed the separation to be for the best. Her parents ordered her to leave Dickens's house, but she refused. She was thirty years old and for fifteen years she had made her home with his family. She was devoted to the children. Perhaps she was even in love with Dickens. When Catherine left Tavistock House Georgina remained. Her decision to stay was to confuse the situation even more. Although her loyalty to Dickens helped to convince some people that the blame for the separation could not all be on his side, it also made others believe that she was the woman who had caused all the trouble.

Dickens was anxious that the separation should not be publicly known, because he believed it could affect his earnings both as a novelist and a reader. A settlement was quickly worked out, with Forster acting for Dickens and Mark Lemon acting for Catherine. Dickens was prepared to be generous and authorised Forster to offer Catherine six hundred pounds a year and a house of her own. On 14 May Lemon "thankfully" accepted on behalf of Catherine.

When Dickens and his wife separated, he was forty-six years old and she was forty-three. They had been married twenty-two years and she had borne him ten children. Nine of the children were living, the eldest was twenty-one and the youngest was six. Dickens asked his eldest son, Charley, to go with his mother in order to protect her. Charley did not want to leave his father, but did so because he believed it to be his duty. Dickens had taken the Ternan family under his protection. Ellen was living with her mother and sisters in lodgings at 31 Berners Street, Oxford Street. There is no evidence that Dickens had been unfaithful to Catherine before the separation and he certainly was not so for some months afterwards.

Up to the agreement over the terms of the settlement, the affair had been handled discreetly. Then Dickens learned that Mrs. Hogarth and her youngest daughter, Helen, were circulating the story that Ellen Ternan was his mistress. He was like a madman in his anger. He refused to make any settlement on Catherine until her mother and sister denied the story formally and in writing. The Hogarths refused because they believed the story to be true. He let them know that unless they signed a full retraction Catherine would not get a penny. They could drag him through every court on earth, but he would not be moved. He was engulfed in a rage that blotted out everything except this quarrel with the Hogarths. It seemed to his daughter Katey that he did not give a damn what happened to anybody else, not even his children. She wrote: "Nothing could surpass the misery and unhappiness of our home."

The Hogarths held out for a fortnight before they yielded. Then on 29 May, 1858, they signed a formal retraction of their statements about Ellen Ternan. They solemnly declared that they now disbelieved such statements and they pledged themselves on all occasions to contradict them.

London was buzzing with rumours. Dickens's name was

linked with Georgina Hogarth, with Ellen Ternan and with the names of other actresses. In the Garrick Club one night Thackeray was told that the separation was caused by a love affair between Dickens and Georgina. "No such thing," Thackeray said, "it's with an actress." His intention was to scotch the more scandalous story, but the remark came back to Dickens, who wrote furiously to Thackeray denying all charges against Ellen Ternan and himself.

To his demented mind it seemed that the whole world must have heard these stories and he resolved to put out a public statement to explain the situation and to silence the scandal. He was in no fit state to make such a decision. Perhaps under other circumstances he would have said nothing, knowing that these rumours would eventually die away. After all, no one had wanted the separation to remain private more than he. But now he had to show himself twice a week at the St. Martin's Hall. Moreover, he was planning a provincial tour for the autumn and he could not bear the thought of his audiences whispering against him. Forster and Lemon, to whom he showed the statement, advised him against publication, but he would not listen. Against Forster's resistance the most he would do was to offer to show the statement to John Delane, editor of *The Times*, and abide by his decision. Unfortunately for Dickens, Delane agreed with him and the statement was published in *Household Words* on 12 June, 1858. It occupied the front page under the heading "PERSONAL".

"Some domestic trouble of mine, of long standing," Dickens told his readers, had "lately been brought to an arrangement" which involved "no anger or ill-will of any kind." By some means this trouble had been made the occasion of misrepresentations, "most grossly false, most monstrous, and most cruel," involving not only him but innocent persons dear to his heart. He believed these slanders to be so widely spread that he doubted if one reader in a thousand had not felt the breath of them, "like an unwholesome air". He solemnly declared that these rumours were "abominably false" and that whosoever repeated one of them after this denial, would lie "as wilfully and as foully as it is possible for any false witness to lie, before Heaven and earth".

Dickens sent copies of this statement to other journals and magazines. It was widely published and most readers were puzzled, for up to now they had known nothing of his troubles.

Five days after the publication of the statement, he had to face the ordeal of appearing at the St. Martin's Hall not certain of his reception by the audience. His friends feared that the indignation caused in some quarters by the statement might be expressed when he made his appearance on the platform. Arthur Smith, his manager, was terrified. Dickens stepped on to the platform, walking rather stiffly, with his right shoulder well forward. He was greeted with a roar of cheers which could be heard a block away from the hall. The cheering was renewed again and again as if the audience could not tell him sufficiently how much they loved him. He showed no emotion. He took his place at the reading desk, opened his book and began to read.

This ovation confirmed him in his belief that throughout the domestic troubles he had been completely in the right, but he still remained bitter and angry. Those who had criticised his behaviour he now regarded as enemies. They included some of his oldest friends, among them Mark Lemon, who had refused to publish the statement in *Punch* on the grounds that it was not suitable for a humorous journal. Bradbury and Evans were the publishers of *Punch*, so Frederick Evans incurred the same enmity. Dickens would not allow the firm to publish any more of his books. As the largest shareholder, he tried to oust them from printing *Household Words*. When he failed in this, he withdrew from the board and the following year started another journal entitled *All the Year Round*. He knew that without his name *Household Words* would have little sale. *All the Year Round* became a great success and, as he intended, it ruined *Household Words*.

The domestic troubles caused the final breach between Thackeray and Dickens. Thackeray's blundering remark still rankled and in June Dickens was given an opportunity to hit out at him. His young friend Edmund Yates had recently published a flippant article on Thackeray which had offended the older man. Thackeray had demanded an apology and Yates came to Dickens for advice. Had Dickens been in his right mind he would have told Yates to apologise, but he was angry and resentful, He told Yates not to apologise, and even drafted his reply to Thackeray. Yates and Thackeray both belonged to the Garrick Club and Thackeray appealed to the committee that Yates's behaviour was intolerable in a member. The "Garrick Club Affair", as it came to be known, caused a rift between those members who supported Thackeray and those who backed Dickens and Yates. At the General Meeting on 10 July the vote went against Yates and he was expelled from the club. The result was a blow to Dickens's prestige and he immediately resigned from the committee.

By 22 July, when he gave the last of the London Readings, the storm that had followed the separation was beginning to die down. Ten days later he set off on a provincial tour, during which he gave eighty-seven Readings and visited forty-two towns.

The tour was a triumph from the very start. It began on 2 August at Clifton in the West Country. Dickens told Collins that on the first night the audience was "perfectly taken off their feet by *The Chimes* – started – looked at each other – started again – looked at me – and then burst into a storm of applause". On the second night there was even more enthusiasm. A local business man said: "Now they know what it is, Mr. Dickens might stay a month and always have a cram." On the final night "a torrent of five hundred shillings bore Arthur away, pounded him against the wall, flowed on to the seats over his body, scratched him, and damaged his best dress suit. All to his unspeakable joy".

Dickens had a great night at Exeter. "It was a prodigious cram and we turned away no end of people." But the prospects at Plymouth did not look so good. There were races and public balls, the Yacht Squadron had gone to Cherbourg, and the hall was badly situated "at the top of a windy and muddy hill, leading (literally) to nowhere". It looked as if "the subsidence of the waters after the Deluge" might have left it there. But the audiences were wonderful. He had never known the minutest touches of *Little Dombey* go better in London and as he read *Boots at the Holly Tree Inn* "the people gave themselves up altogether (Generals, Mayors and Shillings, equally) to a perfect transport of enjoyment of him and the two children". He told Miss Coutts: "It is a great sensation to have an audience in one's hand."

Arthur Smith was doing all he could to make the tour a success. Dickens told Georgina: "He knows only two characters. He is either always corresponding, like a Secretary of State, or he is transformed into a rout-furniture dealer of Rathbone Place, and drags forms about with the greatest violence, without his coat." At Wolverhampton Smith worked like a madman to have the Corn Exchange ready in time for the evening's Reading. At Shrewsbury the hall had no platform, so he set about making one out of tables. "He is all usefulness and service," Dickens told Collins. "I never could have done without him—should have left the unredeemed Bills on the walls and taken flight."

To Collins's joking remark that the hotels in the various towns he visited must afford him many romantic opportunities, Dickens replied: "As to that furtive and Don Giovanni purpose at which you hint, that may be all very well for your violent vigour, or that of the companions with whom you may have travelled continentally, or the Caliph Haroun Alraschid with whom you have unbent metropolitanly; but anchorites who read themselves red hot every night are chaste as Diana (If I suppose *she* was by the bye, but I find I don't quite believe it when I write her name)." He told Collins that he was pleased with the way the tour was going, particularly with the fact that wherever he read the turn-away was invariably greater on the second occasion. "They don't quite understand beforehand what it is, I think, and expect a man to be sitting down in some corner, droning away

Phiz. Sergeant Buzfuz addresses the court (*The Trial from Pickwick*)

Phiz. Pecksniff arouses the street (*Mrs. Gamp*)

like a mild bagpipe." He admitted that he missed the quietness of Gad's Hill. "But perhaps it is best for me not to have it just now, and to wear and toss my storm away – or as much of it as will ever calm down while the water rolls – in this restless manner."

From Chester he went to Liverpool to give four Readings. The receipts for the first two were over one hundred pounds each night, but on the third night the audience numbered two thousand three hundred and the receipts were two hundred guineas. "Arthur bathed in checks, took headers into tickets, floated on billows of passes, dived under weirs of shillings, staggered home, faint with gold and silver." Moreover, this great audience was an appreciative one. "Every point taken. The nicest and finest bits in Little Dombey hitting like chain shot." At Liverpool Dickens and Smith finalised the itinerary for the rest of the tour. It was decided that the tour should finish on 13 November to allow Dickens time to write a story for the Christmas number of *Household Words*.

From Liverpool he sailed to Ireland. In Dublin, where he was to give five Readings, people fought in the agent's shop for tickets. On the first night he read *The Chimes*. When he returned to the hotel, the Boots was waiting for him. "Whaa't sart of hoose, sur?" he asked Dickens. "Capital," Dickens replied. "The Lard be praised for the 'onor o' Dooblin!" said the Boots. The next day the newspapers were filled with reports of the Reading. Dickens told Georgina: "Generally, I am happy to report, the Emerald press is in favour of my appearance, and likes my eyes. But one gentleman comes out with a letter at Cork, wherein he says that although only forty-six I look like an old man. He is a rum customer, I think." He read *Little Dombey* that day and "the crying was universal".

When he set out from his hotel to the Rotunda for the final Dublin Reading, he had to struggle for a mile against the stream of people turned away. At the hall the crowds in the lobbies were so great that he had difficulty getting in. They had broken all the glass in the pay boxes and his men were squeezed against the wall.

E

The hall was so packed that some ladies had to stand all night with their chins against his platform.

In Belfast, where he gave three Readings, the same scenes were repeated. When the doors opened on the first night there was a rush which the police were unable to check. Smith was in the deepest misery because "shillings got into stalls and half-crowns got into shillings, and stalls got nowhere and there was immense confusion". At the Reading of *Little Dombey* Dickens had never seen men cry so openly. He told Georgina: "They made no attempt whatever to hide it, and certainly cried more than the women. As to the Boots at night and Mrs. Gamp too, it was just one roar with me and them, for they made me laugh so that sometimes I *could not* compose my face to go on."

Wherever he went in Ireland he was touched by the personal affection the people had for him. After every performance ladies begged his valet for the flower from his buttonhole. During one of the Readings at Belfast the petals from his geranium showered to the floor and, when he was gone, some ladies mounted the platform and picked them up as keepsakes. Again at Belfast, as he hurried to his hotel after the final Reading, a working man stopped him and said: "Do me the honour to shake hands, Misther Dickens, and God bless you, sir; not ounly for the light you've been to me this night, but for the light you've been in me house, sir (and God love your face!) this many a year."

He left Belfast for Cork, breaking his journey at Dublin. He had been touring for almost four weeks and from Dublin on 29 August he gave Georgina an account of his profits: "For novelty's sake, I will give you some statistics. To understand which, you must be informed that Arthur charges every place with its proportion of the next prospective expenses. For instance, before my profit is declared here, it is debited with the journey to Belfast; and before my profit is declared at Belfast, it is debited in its turn with *its* share of our expenses home to London. After all these deductions, and after paying Arthur's share, I made here £210, and at Belfast (in two days) £130. With a good return at

Cork, and nothing very great at Limerick, from which we don't expect much (except pretty women, for which it is famous), I shall have a handsome Thousand Pounds, since I left Gad's Hill on our country Tour!"

This was an immense profit, considering the heavy expenses of the tour. There were the rents and staffing of the halls to be paid and, in addition to Smith, three people travelled with Dickens; his valet, the gasman and Smith's assistant. The profit could have been even greater had Dickens not stipulated from the start that good seating accommodation must be made available at one shilling for those who could not afford to pay more. He had always been the champion of the working man and he did not want to deprive him of the chance of hearing the Readings.

Cork was not a large city, but a thousand stalls had been booked in advance for the three Readings. At the conclusion of the final Reading the audience rained flowers down on him. Limerick, where he read twice, was too small for his purpose. He told Wills, his associate on *Household Words:* "Arthur says that when he opened the doors last night there was a rush of – three Ducks! We expect a Pig tonight!" From Limerick he travelled back to London.

On arriving in London on Saturday, 4 September, Dickens was dismayed to find that the scandal of the separation had flared up again. The cause was a letter of his which had found its way into the newspapers. He had written this letter at the same time as the public statement and given it to Arthur Smith with instructions to show it to "anyone who wishes to do me right, or to anyone who may have been misled into doing me wrong". At the time he was preparing for the provincial tour and he wanted his business manager to be able to refute any scandalous rumours he might hear.

The letter began: "Mrs. Dickens and I have lived unhappily together for many years. Hardly anyone who has known me intimately can fail to have known that we are, in all respects of character and temperament, wonderfully unsuited to each other. I suppose that no two people not vicious in themselves, ever were joined together, who had a greater difficulty in understanding one another, or who had less in common."

He went on to say that on many occasions nothing had stood between them and a separation but Georgina Hogarth. "From the age of fifteen, she has devoted herself to our home and our children. She has been their playmate, nurse, instructress, friend, protectress, adviser and companion. In the manly consideration towards Mrs. Dickens which I owe to my wife, I will merely remark of her that the peculiarity of her character has thrown all the children on someone else."

"For some years past," he continued, "Mrs. Dickens has been in the habit of representing to me that it would be better for her to go away and live apart, that her always increasing estrangement made a mental disorder under which she sometimes labours – more, that she felt herself unfit for the life she had to lead as my wife and that she would be better far away." He had always replied that they must bear their misfortune for the sake of the children and remain bound together at least in appearance, but recently Forster had suggested that, even for the sake of the children, it would be better for him and his wife to separate.

He referred next to the terms of the settlement. "Of the pecuniary part of them, I will only say that I believe they are as generous as if Mrs. Dickens were a lady of distinction, and I a man of fortune." He hoped that no one could possibly be so cruel and unjust as to put any misconstruction on the separation. "My elder children all understand it perfectly, and all accept it as inevitable. There is not a shadow of doubt or concealment among us – my eldest son and I are one, as to it all."

He turned to the rumours about Ellen Ternan, which had been circulated by Mrs. Hogarth and her daughter. A copy of their signed retraction was attached to the letter. "Two wicked persons who should have spoken very differently of me, in consideration of earned respect and gratitude, have (as I am told, and indeed to

my personal knowledge) coupled with this separation the name
of a young lady for whom I have a great attachment and regard.
I will not repeat her name – I honour it too much. Upon my soul
and honour, there is not on this earth a more virtuous or spotless
creature than this young lady. I know her to be innocent and
pure, and as good as my own dear daughters." He was sure that
Mrs. Dickens, having received this assurance from him, must
now believe it. His children had never doubted him in this
matter. They were certain that he would not deceive them. "All
is open and plain among us, as though we were brothers and
sisters."

Smith had shown this letter to the London correspondent of
the *New York Tribune* and the text was printed in the issue of
16 August. From this it had been widely copied in British newspapers, sometimes with unfavourable comments to the effect
that it was scarcely "manly consideration" on the part of Dickens
to state openly that his wife was indifferent towards her children
and to infer that she might be insane. Dickens was angry that the
letter had got into print, but, in view of the instructions he had
given Smith, he had only himself to blame. He insisted that he had
written the letter as "a private repudiation of monstrous scandals"
and in the future he was always to refer to it as the "violated
letter".

While this publicity raged about him, Dickens was completing
the arrangements for his secret life with Ellen Ternan. In October
he sent her eldest sister, Frances Eleanor, to Italy to complete her
musical education. Her mother went with her. Shortly afterwards
Ellen and Maria moved from the Berners Street lodgings to
No. 2 Houghton Place, Ampthill Square, and probably about this
time Ellen became his mistress. From this time on, their tracks
were so well covered that the most assiduous research has un-
earthed only fragmentary details of their *sub rosa* life together.

As for Catherine, she never once spoke out against the charges
her husband had made against her. She lived quietly, treasuring
the letters he had written to her during their courtship and

marriage, for they proved to her that, despite all that had happened, he had once loved her. For the rest of his life, in his bitterness and guilt, Dickens could never bring himself to speak other than coldly of his wife.

Four days after his return from Ireland he set off for Yorkshire on the next stage of his tour. He was scheduled to read in Huddersfield, Wakefield, York, Harrogate, Scarborough, Hull, Leeds, Halifax and Sheffield, all within the space of nine days. His image had been damaged by the publication of the "violated letter", but this did not have any noticeable effect on his reception. At York he had "a most magnificent assemblage" led by the Archbishop. He could have stayed a week let alone a night. It was in York that he had an encounter which moved him deeply and brought him close to what he sometimes dreamed might be his fame. A lady, whose face he had never seen, stopped him in the street and said: "Mr. Dickens, will you let me touch the hand that has filled my house with many friends?"

He found the spa town of Harrogate "the queerest place with the strangest people in it, leading the oddest lives of dancing, newspaper reading and tables d'hôte." At the Reading of *Little Dombey* one man was completely overcome. After crying a great deal without hiding it, he covered his face with both hands, laid it down on the back of the seat before him and shook with emotion. He was not in mourning, but Dickens supposed him to have lost a child at some time. Also present was a young man, "who found something so very ludicrous in Toots, that he *could not* compose himself at all, but laughed until he sat wiping his eyes with his handkerchief. And whenever he felt Toots coming again he began to laugh and wipe his eyes afresh, as if it were too much for him."

At Hull Dickens had to promise the people that he would come back for two further Readings. They were so excited that he dared not have done otherwise. Smith had his shirt front and waistcoat torn off in the rush. "He was perfectly enraptured in consequence." Halifax, "as horrible a place as I ever saw", was too small for him, but he never had so good an audience. "They were really worth reading to for nothing, though I didn't do exactly that." At Sheffield the run on tickets was so great that Smith had to get posters out announcing that no more could be sold. As it turned out, he could hardly pack into the hall the numbers who had already paid and he advised Dickens to come back at the end of October. Because of the success of the Readings already given, they were now revising the tour list, striking out the smaller towns. At the end of nine hectic days in Yorkshire Dickens was obliged to ask his London chemist to send him a fresh supply of Voice Jujubes and Astringent Lozenges.

It seemed to him that he had been doing nothing all his life except reading, sleeping and travelling in trains. He found the work "sometimes overpowering", but when he was on the platform the warmth of the audience revitalised him. He told Forster: "Sometimes before I go down to read (especially when it is in the day) I am so oppressed by having to do it that I feel perfectly unequal to the task. But the people lift me out of this directly; and I find that I have quite forgotten everything but them and the book, in a quarter of an hour."

He arrived in Manchester to find seven hundred stalls already booked for the one Reading. Dickens was well-liked in Manchester. He had acted there several times with his amateur company and it was one of his favourite towns. That night he read before two thousand five hundred people. The welcome they gave him was outstanding in its affection. When he appeared on the platform, the entire audience rose to their feet and it seemed that the applause and cheering would never be over. He told Forster: "I never saw such a sight or heard such a sound." He knew they were expressing their support and sympathy for him in his domestic troubles and the tears rolled down his cheeks.

From the cotton town of Manchester he travelled to the coal country of the North East, to Darlington, Durham, Sunderland and Newcastle, all bleak industrial towns, with the exception of the cathedral city of Durham, where he read to an audience led by the Dean and Chapter, "humbly followed up by Mayor and local bores". "Little Darlington" covered itself with glory. He read in a "mouldy old Assembly Room without a Lamp abutting on the street, so that I passed it a dozen times and looked for it, when I went down to read". But all sorts of people came in from outlying places "and the town was drunk with the *Carol* far into the night". He read the *Carol* again at Sunderland and did such a number of new things in it that Arthur Smith "stood in amazement at the Wing, and roared and stamped as if it were an entirely new book, topping all the others".

From the North East of England he travelled to Scotland, to Edinburgh, where he read four times during the last week in September. He began with what was for him a poor audience. For the first time on the tour he sensed a coldness connected with the separation, but when he read *The Chimes* the effect was all that he could have wished for. It was the same on the second night with *Little Dombey*. On the third night hundreds upon hundreds of people were turned away. On the final night he read the *Carol*. In the morning posters had announced throughout the city that all the tickets were gone, but this made no difference to the crowds who besieged the hall. They were so great that the police had difficulty in keeping a clear passage to the doors. The Edinburgh Readings were the greatest triumph of the tour. Dickens was especially pleased with this, because of the initial coldness towards him. He told Wills that he considered it a brilliant victory. "The city was taken by storm and carried. The Chimes shook it; Little Dombey blew it up." His profit there was two hundred pounds. His profit for the month of September was nine hundred pounds. "No doubt in reason this sum will have passed £1,000 before I begin the next Thousand in Glasgow."

After Edinburgh he read in Dundee, "an odd place, like Wapping, with high rugged hills behind it". He read in the Corn Exchange, an enormous building that looked "something between the Crystal Palace and Westminster Hall". At Aberdeen the room was "crammed to the street" twice in one day. At Perth, where he thought there literally could be no one to come because the town looked so dead, "the nobility came posting in from thirty miles round" and filled an immense hall.

Wherever he went the people showed their love for him. "I cannot tell you what the demonstrations of personal regard and respect are," he wrote to Forster. "How the densest and most uncomfortably packed crowd will be hushed in an instant when I show my face. How the youth of colleges and the old men of business in the town, seem equally unable to get near enough to me when they cheer me away at night. How common folk and gentlefolk will stop me in the streets . . . And if you saw the mothers, and fathers, and sisters, and brothers in mourning, who invariably come to Little Dombey, and if you studied the wonderful expression of comfort and reliance with which they hang about me, as if I had been with them, all kindness and delicacy, at their own little death-bed, you would think it one of the strangest things in the world."

At Glasgow, where he read four times, the receipts totalled the large sum of six hundred pounds. "As to the effect," he told Forster, "if you had seen them after Lilian died in The Chimes, or when Scrooge woke and talked to the boy outside the window, I doubt if you would ever have forgotten it. And at the end of Little Dombey, yesterday afternoon, in the cold light of day, they all got up, after a short pause, gentle and simple, and thundered and waved their hats with that astonishing heartiness and fondness for me, that for the first time in all my public career they took me completely off my legs, and I saw the whole eighteen hundred of them reel on one side as if a shock from without had shaken the wall."

From Glasgow he travelled southwards to the Midlands. At Birmingham he read *The Trial from Pickwick* and when Sergeant Buzfuz said, "Call Samuel Weller!" the audience gave a round of applause, "as if he were really coming in". At the end of October he returned to Hull and Sheffield for the extra

Readings he had promised. The tour ended at Brighton on 13 November. It had been wonderfully successful. His clear profit, after all deductions and expenses, had been more than a thousand guineas a month. Even more gratifying had been the manner in which people everywhere had expressed their personal affection for him. He told Miss Coutts: "I consider it a remarkable instance of good fortune that it should have fallen out that I should, in this autumn of all others, have come face to face with so many multitudes."

YEARS OF DEPARTED HAPPINESS

THE AUTUMN TOUR of 1858 was followed by a short Christmas season at the St. Martin's Hall. On Christmas Eve, Boxing Day and Twelfth Night he read the *Carol* and the *Pickwick Trial*. So many people were unable to obtain tickets that five extra Readings had to be given in January and February. Then, in the October of 1859, he gave thirteen Readings in ten provincial towns not visited on the first tour. Again these were followed by a Christmas season at the St. Martin's Hall, where he gave three Readings of the *Carol* and the *Pickwick Trial*, the final one taking place on 2 January, 1860. There were no further Readings during 1860, apart from a charity Reading at Chatham on 18 December. Throughout the year Dickens was busy with *Great Expectations*.

By the following spring, however, as the book neared completion, his mind turned again to the prospect of reading. Together with Arthur Smith he planned six London Readings to be followed by a provincial tour. The six readings were given in March and April 1861. They took place at the St. James's Hall because the St. Martin's Hall had been burnt down the previous

August. The St. James's Hall, between Regent Street and Piccadilly, was considerably larger than the St. Martin's Hall, having a seating capacity of two thousand one hundred and twenty-seven. After the final night Dickens told Forster: "The result of the six was, that after paying a large staff of men and all other charges, and Arthur Smith's ten per cent on the receipts, and replacing everything destroyed in the fire at St. Martin's Hall (including all our tickets, country baggage, check-boxes, books, and a quantity of gas-fittings and what not), I got upwards of £500. A very great result. We certainly might have gone on through the season, but I am heartily glad to be concentrated on my story."

He was having difficulty in working out the conclusion of *Great Expectations* and the provincial tour was delayed until he had finished the book. Throughout the writing of the final chapters he was troubled by neuralgia in his face, but the pains left him the moment the book was completed. This made him resolve to do no more writing for some time and it was with relief that he turned to rehearsing his new Readings. He told Forster: "With great pains I have made a continuous narrative out of Copperfield that I think will reward the exertion it is likely to cost me."

The *David Copperfield* Reading opened and closed on the beach at Yarmouth. It began with a happy picture of Mr. Peggotty and his household in the old converted boat. Shortly after Steerforth's introduction to Peggotty's family at the time of Emily's betrothal to Ham, the drift of the story was foreshadowed in his talk with David as they walked back across the sands to their hotel. Steerforth said: "Daisy, – for though that's not the name your godfathers and godmothers gave you, you're such a fresh fellow, that it's the name I best like to call you by – and I wish, I wish, I wish you could give it to me."

The significance of this was soon to be evident as was David's mention of his looking in at Steerforth's bedroom the following morning, before going away, and finding his handsome friend fast asleep, "lying easily with his head upon his arm", as he had often seen him lie in the dormitory at school. "Thus in this silent hour I left him," said Dickens, as David, in mournful tones. "Never more, O God forgive you, Steerforth! to touch that passive hand in love and friendship. Never, never more!" The thrill of the pathos in Dickens's voice reminded his American friend, James T. Fields, of Hazlitt's description of Kean's Othello, "striking on the heart like the swelling notes of some divine music, like the sound of years of departed happiness".

When David next returned to Yarmouth he learned of Steerforth's treachery and his flight with Emily. In this powerful scene Dickens portrayed Ham, with horror-stricken face, whispering, "Emily's run away"; and Mr. Peggotty, dazed by the news, demanding to know the name of the man, then turning to David, the anger in his voice concentrated and controlled, "It's your friend Steerforth and he's a damned villain."

In contrast came the supper at David's chambers, with Traddles and Mr. and Mrs. Micawber as his guests. Dickens swayed backwards and forwards, first on his heels and then on his toes, and there was Mr. Micawber exclaiming, "My dear Copperfield, this is *lux-u-rious*; this is a way of life which reminds me of the period when I was myself in" – the remainder of the sentence seemed to gather in his throat and almost choke him before he managed to gasp out – "a-state-of-celibacy." "As to Mrs. Micawber," Dickens told the audience, "I don't know whether it was the effect of the cap, or the lavender water, or the pins, or the fire, or the wax-candles, but she came out of my room comparatively speaking *l-l-l-lovely*." The prolonging of the initial consonant had a most ludicrous effect. Another hilarious scene was the one between David and Dora when he plucked up the courage to propose to her. Dora's dog, Jip, barked all the time and Dora cried all the time. As David's eloquence increased, so did Jip's barking and Dora's crying, the three of them becoming more demented every minute.

The Reading ended with an evocative description of the great storm in which Steerforth perished. In the dying storm a fisherman led David to the shore. "And on that part of it where she and I had looked for shells, two children – on that part of it where some lighter fragments of the old boat, blown down last night, had been scattered by the wind – among the ruins of the home he had wronged – I saw *him* lying with his head upon his arm, as I had often seen him lie at school."

The *David Copperfield* Reading was to become a great favourite both with audiences and with Dickens. His dependence on the support of his audience was evident in this Reading because of its length and its difficulty. If this support were lacking, the Reading flagged, especially during the description of the storm.

Dickens had also prepared a Reading from *Nicholas Nickleby* based on the episodes at Dotheboy's Hall. He scored a great hit with his impersonation of Mr. Wackford Squeers, the rascally principal. The audience first met Squeers in the coffee-room of the Saracen's Head enjoying his hot toast and cold round of beef, while five little boys sat miserably opposite waiting for their share of twopenn'orth of milk and thick bread and butter for three. He admonished them, with a chuckle, "Conquer your passions, boys, and don't be eager after vittles."

A favourite scene with audiences was the one when Squeers read to the assembled pupils the letters received from their parents and guardians. He first gained attention with a ferocious slap on the desk. "Graymarsh, he's the next. Stand up, Graymarsh! Graymarsh's maternal aunt is very glad to hear he's so well and happy, and sends her respectful compliments to Mrs. Squeers, and thinks she must be a *han*gel. She likewise thinks Mr. Squeers is too good for this world, but hopes he may long be spared to carry on the business. Would have sent two pairs of stockings, as desired, but is short of money and forwards a tract instead. Hopes above all that he will study in everything to please Mr. and Mrs. Squeers, and look upon them as his only friends; and that he will love Master Squeers; and not object to sleeping five in a bed, which no Christian should. Ah! a delightful letter; very affecting, indeed."

Dickens made Squeers add in the Reading, but not in the novel, "A good man struggling with his destiny is – a spectacle for things in general." This is one of several interpolations in the Reading. In addressing his class "in English spelling and philosophy", Mr. Squeers defined a horse as "a quadruped; and quadruped's Latin, *or Greek, or Hebrew, or some other language that's dead and deserves to be*, for beast." None of the italicised words appear in the book. The longest interpolation is Squeers's suggestion to Nicholas about the toilet arrangements. Squeers turned to Nicholas and asked, "Do you wash?" "Occasionally," was the astonished reply. "Umph! I don't know what towel to put you on. I know there's a place on somebody's towel; but if you'll make shift with your pocket handkerchief tomorrow morning, Mrs. Squeers will arrange that in the course of the day." Again, none of this appears in the book.

The final scene was the most dramatic, when Squeers dragged in the wretched Smike to be punished in front of the entire school. "Stand out of the way, Mrs. Squeers, my dear," he said over his shoulder, with a look of delight. "I've hardly got room enough." One blow had fallen on Smike when Nicholas cried, "STOP!" The suddenness and authority of Dickens's voice startled every member of the audience. In the exchange that followed between Nicholas and Squeers the alternation of the characters was astonishingly rapid, but even this had been surpassed in an earlier scene between Nicholas and Fanny Squeers, when it seemed to the audience that one half of Dickens's face was Nicholas and the other half was Fanny.

In addition to *David Copperfield* and *Nicholas Nickleby* Dickens also prepared another Reading for the provincial tour, *Mr. Chops, the Dwarf*, adapted from a Christmas story published in 1858. *Mr. Chops, the Dwarf* was the shortest of all the Readings. Dickens, as Mr. Magsman, told the story of Mr. Chops and how he used to sit on his barrel organ dreaming of the day when he would Come into his Property. He wins twelve thousand pounds in a lottery and not only Comes into his Property but Goes into

Society. The Reading proved to be too slight and, after a few performances, it was dropped from the repertoire.

The provincial tour was to start at Norwich on 28 October, 1861, and was to be confined to England and Scotland. Many towns not visited previously were included on the list. Then, in the middle of all the preparations, Arthur Smith fell dangerously ill and it was obvious that he would not be fit to manage the tour. In his place, Dickens engaged Thomas Headland, formerly on the staff of the St. Martin's Hall, who had assisted Smith during the Readings there. A visit to Smith at the end of September convinced Dickens that there was little hope of his recovery. He told Forster: "And yet his wakings and wanderings so perpetually turn on his arrangements for the Readings, and he is so desperately unwilling to relinquish the idea of 'going on with the business' tomorrow and tomorrow and tomorrow, that I had not the heart to press him for the papers. He told me that he believed he had by him '70 or 80 letters unanswered'. You may imagine how anxious it makes me, and at what a dead stop I am."

Smith died in October and Dickens grieved over the loss of his loyal manager and close friend. He was utterly depressed at the prospect of touring without him. He told Forster: "With what difficulty I get myself back to the Readings after all this loss and trouble, or with what unwillingness I work myself up to the mark of looking them in the face, I can hardly say. As for poor Arthur Smith at this time, it is as if my right arm were gone. It is only just now that I am able to open one of the books, and screw the text out of myself in a flat dull way."

The first night at Norwich was a dismal beginning to the tour. The hall was cold, Dickens was out of sorts and the audience appeared to be afraid of him and of each other. Without Smith, everything seemed forlorn and strange. But the second night was completely different. He read *Nicholas Nickleby* for the first time. "There was a brilliant audience," he told Collins, "and I think I must report of Nickleby that, for a certain fantastic and hearty

"Why did he die before his poor old, crazy servant!" ~~wringing his clasping his hands and looking up in anguish~~ "Take him from me, and what remains? I loved him. He was good to me. ~~We learnt Tare and Tret together at school.~~ I 5 took him down once, six boys, in the arithmetic class ~at school~. God forgive me! Had I the heart to take him down!"

"Come, Mr. Chuffey," said Pecksniff, "come with me! Summon up your fortitude, Mr. 10 Chuffey."

"Yes, I will. Yes. I'll sum up my forty—Oh, Mr. Chuzzlewit! Oh, my dead master!"

~~He yielded to the hand that guided him, and submitted to be led away.~~ 15

"Well, I'm sure," said Mrs. Gamp, ~~looking scornfully down on him~~; "you're a wearing old soul, and that's the ~~sacred~~ *blessed* truth. It's a pity you don't know wot you say, for you'd tire your own pagienge out if 20 you did, and fret yourself into a happy releage for all as knows you; ~~which ~~

You ought to know that you was born in a wale, and that you live in a wale, and that you must take the consequences of sich a situation

A page from Dickens's prompt copy of *Mrs. Gamp*

Phiz. Betsey Prig and Mrs. Gamp (*Mrs. Gamp*)

enjoyment, it tops all the Readings. The people were really quite ridiculous to see when Squeers read the boys' letters." He had another fine audience on the following night at Bury St. Edmunds, when he gave the first Reading of *David Copperfield*. "I don't think a word – not to say an idea – was lost; and I am confirmed in my impressions that it will be a very great card indeed in London."

From Brighton he told Georgina: "We have been doing tremendously. We turned away half Hastings last night; turned away half Dover; have (for the three Readings) 800 stalls in all already let here, and there will no doubt be 1,000." From a financial point of view all this was very satisfactory, but, without Smith, the tour that was to have been so pleasurable was proving to be nothing more than a grind. He missed him dreadfully. "It is not only that his loss to me socially is quite irreparable, but that the sense I used to have of compactness and comfort about me while I was reading is quite gone. And when I come out for the ten minutes, when I used to find him always ready for me with something cheerful to say, it is forlorn."

Moreover, he was beginning to realise that his new manager, Headland, was inefficient. There had been evidence of mis-management in the towns so far visited, but the first real alarm was over the arrangements for Newcastle upon Tyne, where he was scheduled to read during the third week in November. He was in Brighton when he learned that all the posters advertising the Newcastle Readings had, in some way, been lost on the road. He recalled that the same thing had happened the previous week at Ipswich. It was discovered eventually that all the Newcastle posters, instead of being delivered to the local agent, had been sent to the hall where Dickens was to read, and they were found lying there unopened in a cellar. Headland blamed the London printer who had dispatched them.

The matter appeared to have been put right, but Dickens was still uneasy. When he arrived in Newcastle he was annoyed to find that, although the posters were now displayed all over the

F

town, the wrong Readings were advertised. He was announced to read *Little Dombey* and the *Pickwick Trial* at the final performance and he had instructed Headland to advertise *Copperfield* for that day. He was to read *Copperfield* on the Thursday and he knew it would create a big demand for seats on the Saturday.

Then, in Newcastle, Dickens had a letter from the agent in Edinburgh, where he was to begin reading the following Wednesday. The agent told him that he had not yet received the tickets and posters expected from the printer, and that while all Edinburgh ought to be acquainted with every detail of the Readings, nothing whatever was known. Again Headland blamed the printer, but Dickens could not see how the printer could be always making mistakes now when he had never made them before. "I do not know what is to be done," he told Wills. "It is too plain that the business is awfully mismanaged, and I cannot see my way to putting it right. I am so perfectly helpless in the matter: having my own hard work in it to do, and having of course supposed all these things to be done already."

The local agent in Newcastle complained to Dickens that he had been absolutely powerless when he ought to have been busiest. Jenny Lind, the Swedish soprano, had recently visited the town and when he was sending her circulars out he ought to have been sending Dickens's, but he had none to send. Dickens told Wills: "If all these rooms at all these places in the List were not taken, I would not go on. But the mischief is, that I *must* go on."

On the first night at Newcastle, when he read *Copperfield*, the numbers were about half what they should have been, but the following night the hall was packed. And on this night a terrible tragedy was narrowly averted. During the *Nickleby* Reading, the gas batten over the platform came crashing down with such a noise that it seemed as though the roof were falling. There were three galleries crammed with people and approached by a steep flight of stairs. In a panic many could have fallen and been trampled underfoot. A lady in the front row of the stalls screamed and ran wildly towards Dickens. For an instant there was a frightening surge in the crowd. Dickens was quick to notice that the lady was in full sight of the audience, so he smiled and called out to her pleasantly, as if this happened every night: "There's nothing the matter, I assure you; don't be alarmed; pray sit down." The lady returned to her seat and there was a thunder of applause. The batten took some minutes to mend and Dickens looked on with his hands in his pockets. The danger seemed to be over; but he thought that if he left the platform, or turned his back for a moment, there might still be a panic. His men were alarmed, for they knew that the whole place might have taken fire. His valet said afterwards: "but there stood the master as cool as ever I see him a-lounging at a railway station."

Dickens left Newcastle for Edinburgh, breaking the journey at Berwick-on-Tweed, where he was to read for one night. It was a small town for him to read in, but had been included on Arthur Smith's principle that a place on the way paid the expenses of a through journey. When he arrived in Edinburgh he was relieved to find the posters had been located and distributed. On the first night the audience was exactly double what it had been on the first night the last time, when he had been received so coldly. He had a wonderful success with *Copperfield*. He told Wills: "The impression on the audience, without precedent in the reading chronicles. Four rounds when I went in – laughing and crying and thundering all the time – and a great burst of cheering at last. They lost nothing – not the minutest detail – and I almost think it would have been better to have done Copperfield every night."

The following night, "in a gale of wind and a fierce rain", a thousand people were turned away. He told his daughter Mamie: "There was no getting into the hall, no getting near the hall, no stirring among the people, no getting out, no possibility of getting rid of them. And yet, in spite of all that, and of their being steaming wet, they never flagged for an instant, never made a complaint, and took up the Trial upon their very shoulders, to the last word, in a triumphant roar."

An even greater crowd turned up for the final Reading, when, through the incompetence of Headland, the number of tickets issued was out of all proportion to the space available. Dickens went on to the platform at the usual time and found himself facing not an audience but a mob, which overflowed into the passages and the streets and was increasing all the time as the crowds outside forced a great turbid stream of people into the already crammed hall. His appearance on the platform had a calming effect and in the comparative quiet he told them how sorry he was that this had happened, that he would do anything to set it right, and that he would alter his arrangements and come back and read to all Edinburgh if they wished. During this speech the people inside the hall were quiet, but he could hear the dim reverberations of the roars of the crowd outside. At the end of his speech there was great cheering and a voice cried: "Go on, Mr. Dickens. Everybody will be quiet now." This was followed by a shout: "*We won't* be quiet. We won't let the Reading be heard. We're ill-treated." Dickens said: "There's plenty of time and you may rely upon it that the Reading is in no danger of being heard until we are agreed." And he good-humouredly shut up his book. There was great applause and then everyone became quiet.

In the dead silence Dickens prepared to read, when a gentleman, with a lady on his arm, whose dress had been torn to ribbons, cried out: "Mr. Dickens! – Sir – Couldn't some people, at all events, ladies, be accommodated on your platform?" "Most certainly," Dickens replied. At this there was loud cheering. "Which way can they come to the platform, Mr. Dickens?" "Round here to my left." To everyone who came up he said in a low voice how sorry he was and they smiled and said it was nothing. But when all the people were on the platform, the rest of the audience began to shout, because they could not see Dickens. At least half the people on the platform were ladies and he suggested to them that they sit down or lie down. Instantly they all dropped into recumbent groups, with Dickens standing up in the centre. He told Wills: "I don't know what it looked like most – a battlefield – an impossible tableau – a gigantic picnic. There was one very pretty girl in full dress lying down on her side all night, and holding on to one leg of my table. So I read Nickleby and the Trial. From the beginning to the end they didn't lose one point, and they ended with a great burst of cheering."

From Edinburgh he travelled to Glasgow and then southwards through Carlisle, Lancaster and Preston to Manchester. On Saturday, 14 December, the Prince Consort died. Dickens was scheduled to read in Liverpool the following week, but because of the Prince's death the Mayor of Liverpool recommended that the Readings be cancelled. From Manchester Dickens travelled home to Gad's Hill.

After a short Christmas break he set off on 30 December for the Midlands. At Cheltenham Macready came to hear him read *Copperfield*. Afterwards the old actor told him, with tears running down his face, that "as a piece of art it – er – laid him on his – er – back; and that as a piece of passion and pathos and playfulness, it – er – well! – there was nothing to be said about it. N–no, Dickens, Nothing!" *Copperfield* was the great hit of the tour and in the reading of it Dickens was taking as much out of himself as he had done in the part of Richard Wardour in *The Frozen Deep*.

The tour should have ended by the middle of January, but he had postponed five Readings in Liverpool and neighbourhood on account of the Prince Consort's death and now he had to work them out. On 30 January, 1862, he completely finished the provincial Readings. He had visited twenty-four towns and given forty-three Readings. He told his friend Thomas Beard: "The brilliancy of the close – at Manchester and Liverpool – has been absolutely dazzling."

The provincial tour was followed by twelve Readings at the St. James's Hall beginning 13 March. On the opening night he read *Copperfield* for the first time in London, followed by *Bob Sawyer's Party* to finish the evening merrily. The success of

Copperfield was astounding. It seemed to take everyone by sur-
prise. Although he had looked forward throughout the provincial
tour to the Reading being a London sensation, the reception of it
went beyond his hopes. He had never before seen so excited an
audience, but he admitted that he felt "half-dead" when he had
done reading it.

He finished the London Readings on 27 June. Their success
throughout had been complete. He told Forster: "It seems almost
suicidal to leave off with the town so full, but I don't like to
depart from my public pledge. A man from Australia is in London
ready to pay £10,000 for eight months there."

When this offer was substantially increased, Dickens thought
very seriously of going to Australia. He believed that he might
find there material for a book. This was important to him, for he
was about to start a twenty-number story. He had chosen the
title for this, *Our Mutual Friend*, but he doubted if he could
sustain his invention throughout twenty numbers. Moreover, the
money he would get in Australia would offset any losses through
the failure of his literary powers; but still he hesitated. He told
Forster: "If it was not for the hope of a gain that would make me
more independent of the worst, I could not look the travel and
absence and exertion in the face. I know perfectly well beforehand
how unspeakably wretched I should be. But these renewed and
larger offers tempt me. I can force myself to go aboard a ship, and
I can force myself to do at that reading desk what I have done a
hundred times; but whether with, all this unsettled fluctuating
distress in my mind, I could force an original book out of it, is
another question."

There were strong reasons for making the journey. He was
faced with the question of finding fresh audiences. He had toured
Britain twice within four years. Where else was he to go? The
Civil War had closed America to him. These thoughts were in his
mind when he told Forster: "Remember that at home here, the
thing has never missed fire, but invariably does more the second
time than it did the first; and also that I have got so used to it, and

have worked so hard at it, as to get out of it more than I ever thought was in it for that purpose. I think all the probabilities for such a country as Australia are immense."

He was in a dilemma. He had always been conscious of the needs of his family and, considering the large sum of money he would earn in Australia, he would be doing his duty by them were he to go. On the other hand, he did not want to leave Ellen Ternan and he could not see how he could possibly arrange to take her with him. In the autumn he was still struggling with these arguments. He told Forster: "It is useless and needless for me to say what the conflict in my own mind is. How painfully unwilling I am to go, and yet how painfully sensible that perhaps I ought to go – with all the hands upon my skirts that I cannot fail to feel and see there, whenever I look round. It is a struggle of no common sort, as you will suppose, you who know the circumstances of the struggler."

The struggle ended when he began to see his way through the difficulties of his new book. This made him decide to remain in England. He was writing well and, with this surge of invention, he felt more hopeful and in better spirits than at any time since the separation.

In January, 1863, he went to Paris, where he read at the Embassy in aid of the British Charitable Fund. The Reading was so successful that he consented to read twice again. "Blazes of Triumph!" he reported to Wills. "The curiosity and interest and general buzz about it are quite indescribable. They are so extraordinarily quick to understand a face and gesture going together, that one of the most remarkable points is, that people who don't understand English, positively understand the Readings!"

This was especially evident during the Reading of *Copperfield*. When Dickens as Steerforth gave a cordial grasp of the hand to Mr. Peggotty, saying, "Mr. Peggotty, you are a thoroughly good fellow, and deserve to be as happy as you are tonight. My hand upon it!" then turned and in a different tone offered his hand to young Ham, saying, "Ham, I give you joy, my boy. My hand upon that too!" he heard the low exclamation "Ah-h," from his audience, who had immediately apprehended the situation. When Emily's letter was read, "a low murmur of irrepressible emotion went about like a sort of sea". When David proposed to Dora, "gorgeous beauties all radiant with diamonds, clasped their tans between their two hands and rolled about in ecstasy". The audience listened to his description of the great storm "as if they were in it".

As for the *Pickwick Trial*, their perception of the witnesses, and particularly of Mr. Winkle, was astonishing; and whenever they saw the little Judge coming in, they nudged one another and laughed, "with that amazing relish that I could hardly help laughing as much myself". All these triumphs culminated on the last night, "when they positively applauded and called out expressions of delight, out of the room into the cloak room, out of the cloak room into their carriages, and in their carriages away down the Faubourg".

The brilliant success of the Paris Readings had been widely reported in the London newspapers, so Dickens decided to take advantage of this. He instructed Headland – whom he now referred to privately as Blockheadland – to begin preparations for a short series of Readings at the St. James's Hall. Between March and June thirteen Readings were given. At the end of March, for the sake of the finer effects in the *Copperfield* Reading, he transferred from the St. James's Hall to the smaller Hanover Square Rooms.

The Readings at the Hanover Square Rooms were probably the finest he ever gave. The acoustics were so perfect that the least inflection of his voice could be heard anywhere in the auditorium. Rarely in the future was he to read under such perfect conditions or with such feelings of mental repose and physical well-being. Between these Readings and the next, grief and sickness were to intervene.

Ellen Ternan was travelling with him when the accident occurred. About this time he was dividing his life between Gad's Hill and Elizabeth Cottage, Slough, where Ellen and he lived secretly under the names of Mr. and Mrs. John Tringham. At Staplehurst the train ran into a gap made during a repair to the line. Eight coaches crashed over the bridge into the bed of the river. Ten passengers were killed and many seriously injured. Dickens had a miraculous escape. He was in the only carriage that did not go down, but hung in the air, over the side of the broken bridge.

He managed to get out of the carriage and climbed down to the wreckage. He filled his hat with water and went among the injured. He came upon a staggering man covered with blood from a frightful cut across the skull. He laid him down on the grass, poured water over his face and gave him some brandy. The man said, "I am gone", and died. He stumbled over a lady lying on her back against a tree. Her face was the colour of lead and little streams of blood flowed from her head. He asked her if she could swallow some brandy and she nodded. He gave her a sip and left her for somebody else. The next time he passed her she was dead. He moved to the wreckage where people were screaming for help. They were crushed beneath tremendous weights or twisted among iron, wood, mud and water. He risked his life in his attempts to get them out and in recognition of his heroism he was later presented with a piece of plate by the South Eastern Railway. He was terribly shaken by the accident and for several days after he could not write for the tremors in his hand.

No sooner had he completed *Our Mutual Friend* than his mind turned again for distraction to the Public Readings. Since the last series he was constantly receiving requests to read, but had been reluctant to do so because of the anxieties caused to him then by Headland's mismanagement. He was especially concerned because the blame for any shortcomings in the arrangements had been laid by the public not on Headland but on himself. Early in 1866, however, he saw a way out of this difficulty. He approached Messrs. Chappell of New Bond Street, the concert agents and one of the main shareholders in the company that owned the St. James's Hall. He told them that he was willing to resume the Readings if an agreement could be reached which would relieve him of all business cares connected with them. If this could be arranged, he was willing to negotiate with the firm for a series of about thirty Readings in London and the provinces.

Chappells jumped at this opportunity and the result of the negotiations was that Dickens agreed to give thirty Readings for one thousand five hundred pounds, which worked out at fifty pounds a Reading. Chappells undertook all responsibility and the paying of all expenses, personal and otherwise, including any servants he might take with him. This agreement would relieve Dickens of all business anxieties, leaving him free to concern himself solely with reading, a freedom he had not enjoyed since the death of Arthur Smith.

While these negotiations were proceeding, Dickens had been feeling unwell. His doctor, Frank Beard, gave him a thorough medical examination and diagnosed the trouble as "want of muscular power in the heart". Dr. Brinton, who had been called in for consultation, thought the condition to be "only remarkable irritability of the heart". They prescribed a tonic of iron, quinine and digitalis to send the blood more quickly through the system. Dickens was not disconcerted by the opinions of his doctors. He told Forster: "Of course I am not so foolish as to suppose that all my work can be achieved without *some* penalty, and I have noticed for some time a decided change in my buoyancy and hopefulness – in other words in my usual 'tone'. But the tonics have already brought me round. So I have accepted an offer from Chappells of Bond Street of £50 for thirty nights."

Forster was concerned that this letter telling him of Dickens's illness also announced his decision to go on a hectic Reading tour, with all the physical tiredness and mental excitement this entailed. But Dickens assured him: "As to the Readings, all I have to do is, to take in my book and read, at the appointed place and hour, and come out again. All the business of every kind is done by

Chappells. They take John and my other man, merely for my convenience. I have no more to do with any detail whatever than you have. They transact all the business at their own cost, and on their own responsibility. I think they are disposed to do it in a very good spirit, because whereas the original proposition was for thirty Readings 'in England, Ireland, Scotland, or Paris,' they wrote out in their agreement 'in London, the Provinces, or elsewhere as you and we may agree'."

It was almost three years since he had last read publicly, so he set about practising the Readings. Some idea of the high professional standard he brought to them is given in a letter to Forster: "You have no idea how I have worked at them. Finding it necessary, as their reputation widened, that they should be better than at first, I have *learnt them all*, so as to have no mechanical drawback in looking after the words. I have tested all the serious passion in them by everything I know; made the humorous points much more humorous; corrected my utterance of certain words; cultivated a self-possession not to be disturbed; and made myself master of the situation." He learned them by going over them to himself, "often twice a day, with exactly the same pains as at night, over and over and over again".

In addition to learning his old Readings, he had prepared a new one from *Doctor Marigold's Prescriptions*, a collection of tales which had been published the previous December as the Christmas number of *All the Year Round*. This had proved to be one of his most successful Christmas numbers, the sale exceeding a quarter of a million copies in the first week. To test its suitability as a Reading, he gave a private performance to a group of friends on 18 March, including Wilkie Collins, Robert Browning and Charles Kent.

In the Reading Doctor Marigold, a middle-aged cheap jack, relates the story of his life. He was born on the highway and named "Doctor" as a compliment to the man-midwife who delivered him. He married and had one child, a little girl, but lost both wife and daughter, and continued his travels alone. Coming across a deaf-and-dumb child who resembled his daughter, he adopted her and sent her to a school for deaf mutes to be educated. He lost her when she married a young man, also deaf and dumb, and sailed with him for China. After an absence of a few years she returned, bringing with her a little daughter who could both hear and speak. When Doctor Marigold heard the child talking, tears of joy rolled down his face.

Doctor Marigold was one of the most comic and also one of the most pathetic of the Readings. From the beginning Dickens was the cheap jack, standing on his cart in the market-place of some country town, capturing his audience with the volubility and rapidity of his patter.

"Here's a pair of razors that'll shave you closer than the board of guardians; here's a flat iron worth its weight in gold; here's a frying pan artificially flavoured with essence of beefsteaks to that degree that you've only got for the rest of your lives to fry bread and dripping in it and there you are replete with animal food; here's a genuine chronometer-watch, in such a solid silver case that you may knock at the door with it when you come home late from a social meeting and rouse your wife and family and save up your knocker for the postman; and here's half-a-dozen dinner-plates that you may play the cymbals with to charm the baby when it's fractious. Stop! I'll throw you in another article, and I'll give you that, and it's a rolling-pin; and if the baby can only get it well into its mouth when its teeth is coming and rub the gums once with it, they'll come through double in a fit of laughter equal to being tickled . . ." One after the other the conceits came tumbling out in an inexhaustible sequence. Sometimes there were tears behind the laughter, especially in the scene when Doctor Marigold's little daughter, lying sick across his back, died, while he was convulsing a country audience with his patter.

In the course of his story Doctor Marigold introduced some of his companions on the road. There was Pickleson, an amiable giant, who exhibited under the name of Rinaldo di Velasco. "He was a languid young man," said Dickens as Doctor Marigold, "which I attributed to the distance betwixt his extremities. He had a little head and less in it, he had weak eyes and weak knees, and altogether you couldn't look at him without feeling there was greatly too much of him both for his joints and his mind." Pickleson was managed by the showman, Mim, who was a ferocious swearer and had a very hoarse voice. It was Mim who had given the deaf-and-dumb child to Doctor Marigold in exchange for half-a-dozen pairs of braces. Dickens's high falsetto, when speaking as Pickleson, whose voice, as Doctor Marigold remarked, seemed to come from his eyebrows, and his guttural growlings as Mim were among the funniest parts of the Reading.

But, above all, it was Doctor Marigold's patter that stole the show. "What is it? Why, I'll tell you! It's made of fine gold and it's not broke, though there's a hole in the middle of it, and it's stronger than any fetter that was ever forged. What else is it? I'll tell you. It's a hoop of solid gold wrapped in a silver curl-paper that I myself took off the shining locks of the ever-beautiful old lady in Threadneedle Street, London city. I wouldn't tell you so, if I hadn't the paper to show, or you mightn't believe it even of me. Now, what else is it? It's a man-trap, and a hand-cuff, the parish-stocks and a leg-lock, all in one. Now, what else is it? It's a wedding-ring!" The Reading ended, but Doctor Marigold's patter would never be done. It would go on and on in a never-ending litany, down the years, echoing among the stars, praising God for the wonderful gift of speech.

Even those present at the private Reading who appreciated Dickens's superb talents as an actor were astonished by the extra-ordinary ease and fluency with which he delivered the cheap jack's patter. Dickens explained this in a remark he made to Charles Kent after the Reading. "There!" he said. "If I have gone through that already to myself once, I have gone through it two-hundred-times!"

The opening Reading, under Chappells' management, was given in the St. James's Hall on Tuesday, 10 April, 1866. In addition to the interest created by Dickens's re-appearance on the

platform after so long an absence, there was much excitement
when it was known that he had decided to read *Doctor Marigold*
for the first time on this occasion. *Doctor Marigold* was to be as
great a success as a Reading as it was as a Christmas story. It was
to be the sensation of the third series as *David Copperfield* had been
the sensation of the second.

Chappells had appointed as their representative and manager a
man named George Dolby. To Dickens's relief, Dolby turned out
to be as efficient as Arthur Smith, although he had not the same
social graces. Dolby was tall, bald, imperturbable and wonderfully thick-skinned, with a loud laugh, a stock of jokes and a
tendency to slap people on the back. He was to get on well with
the Americans. Mark Twain called him "a gladsome gorilla".
This vulgar and kindly man became one of Dickens's closest
friends. They were attracted to each other from the moment they
first met. Dolby was devoted to his "Chief" as he invariably
termed Dickens.

On the morning following the London Reading, Dickens and
Dolby strode along the railway platform towards the train that
was to take them to Liverpool, the first stop on the tour. This was
the first of the innumerable railway platforms they were to walk
along together. Dickens was wearing his travelling clothes;
reefer jacket and blue sailor's trousers under his cloak and a soft
wide-brimmed hat pulled down jauntily over one side of his head.
With his wiry moustache and grizzled beard, lined face and
brilliant eyes, he looked, to Dolby, like a gentlemanly pirate. It
was on this journey to Liverpool that Dolby first noticed the look
of anxiety he was always to see on Dickens's face whenever a
train was moving at speed. Dickens told him that since the
Staplehurst accident he could not travel on a fast train without
experiencing a nervous terror.

The tour was even more successful than the two previous ones,
but the fatigue was correspondingly greater, and every one of
Dickens's letters that reported a triumph recorded also a stage in
the deterioration of his health. At Manchester the audience stood

cheering and refused to go home. He told Georgina: "I am, of course, tired (the pull of Marigold upon one's energy, in the Free Trade Hall, was great); but I stick to my tonic, and feel, all things considered, in very good tone." At the second Reading at Liverpool, on the 13 April, the police officially reported that three thousand people were turned away from the hall. He told Mamie: "Except that I cannot sleep, I really think myself in much better training than I had anticipated. A dozen oysters and a little champagne between the parts every night, constitute the best restorative I have ever tried."

At Glasgow the applause was staggering in its volume and his men stood in the wings, checking off his reception by the minute hand of a watch and thinking he would never be allowed to begin. He told Mamie: "I was dead beat afterwards, but plucked up again." From Clifton on 11 May he told Georgina: "It has been very heavy work, getting up at six-thirty each morning after a heavy night, and I am not at all well today. We had a tremendous hall at Birmingham last night, £230 odd, 2,100 people . . . I have so severe a pain in the ball of my left eye that it makes it hard for me to do anything after 100 miles shaking since breakfast. My cold is no better, nor my hand either." The tour ended on 12 June at the St. James's Hall, where the Reading, "in deference to the general desire", was *Doctor Marigold*.

Throughout the tour Dolby had been impressed by Dickens's determination to ensure that any performance he gave would never fall below the high standard he had set himself. Dickens always insisted on testing the acoustics of a hall in which he had never read before. He did this by standing on the platform, while Dolby prowled into every corner and a conversation in low tones was carried on between them. He always stayed in the same hotel as his manager and refused all invitations to dine at private houses, even when these came from close friends. By holding invariably to this routine, the wear and tear of the touring life was considerably reduced, allowing him always to be able to give of his best to his public. He could not bear the thought of letting his

The cover of one of the Reading Editions

Phiz. Little Dombey leaves Doctor Blimber's Academy (*The Story of Little Dombey*)

public down in any way whatsoever. An instance of this was seen at Birmingham, where, by mistake, he finished the Reading with *Nickleby* instead of the *Pickwick Trial* as advertised. The moment this was pointed out to him he returned to the platform, apologised to the audience, and although he was worn out after reading for two hours, he gave them the *Pickwick Trial*.

Chappells had no reason to regret the bargain they had made with Dickens. The gross receipts of the tour amounted to approximately four thousand five hundred pounds, an average of one hundred and fifty pounds a Reading. This could have been more, but Dickens had stipulated, as he had in the two previous tours, that shilling seats must be made available for working people. Some weeks before the Readings closed Chappells had already approached him with an offer of fifty more nights to begin the following year. This time he meant to ask for more than fifty pounds a Reading. He told Forster: "The Chappells are speculators, though of the worthiest and most honourable kind. They make some bad speculations, and have made a very good one in this case, and will set this against those. I told them when we agreed: 'I offer these thirty Readings to you at fifty pounds a night, because I know perfectly well beforehand that no one in your business has the least idea of their real worth, and I wish to prove it.'" At first he was prepared to read forty times at sixty pounds a night, with all expenses paid as before. Then, to make the contract a round sum of money, he suggested reading forty-two times for two thousand five hundred pounds. These terms were agreed on 14 August. The number of Readings was later increased to fifty.

In September Dickens was ill again, this time with stomach pains and heart seizures, but not only did he press on with the writing of *Mugby Junction*, a collection of stories for the Christmas number of *All the Year Round*, but he also adapted two of these stories as Readings for the forthcoming tour. At Christmas he gave a private Reading of these at Gad's Hill to a group of friends Dickens read them well, but the subjects themselves were not worthwhile and those present heard them with misgivings.

Barbox Brothers and *The Boy at Mugby* were to be read as a double bill. Their chief merit lay in the vivid picture they gave of Rugby, the great central junction of the entire railway system of England; the junction which Dickens on his tours had come to know only too well. The hero of *Barbox Brothers* was Mr. Jackson, a middle-aged and bitter man, who resolved to abandon all thoughts of a fixed home and spend the rest of his life in travelling, hoping to find relief in a constant change of scene. On a sudden impulse he got out of his train one night at Mugby Junction and found himself, at three o'clock in the morning, on a windy platform in a drenching rainstorm. For the railways this was "their deadest and buriedest time", the blackest interval between midnight and daybreak, the silence occasionally broken by "mysterious goods trains, covered with palls and gliding on like vast weird funerals, conveying themselves guiltily away, as if their freight had come to a severe and unlawful end". He accepted the invitation of "Lamps", a railway worker, to share the warmth of his little room. Later he met Lamps's daughter, Phoebe, a crippled bed-ridden girl. The love of the father and the daughter for each other awoke his better nature and eventually he forgave the two people who had wronged him in the past.

The Boy at Mugby was based on an incident that actually occurred in the refreshment room at Rugby Junction. Dickens and his associate, Wills, who was travelling with him at the time, had each asked for a cup of coffee, which the lady behind the counter supplied to them. While Wills was feeling in his pocket for some money, Dickens reached across the counter for the sugar and milk, when the lady snatched both articles from him with the remark: "You sha'n't have any milk and sugar till you two fellows have paid for your coffee." At which a small page boy, overjoyed by their discomfiture, burst into an uncontrollable fit of laughter. The two travellers left their coffee on the counter, after an apology for making free with the milk and sugar. But it was an evil day for that page, because he later figured as *The Boy at Mugby*.

Dickens as the Boy described precisely where he was to be found. "Up in a corner of the Down Refreshment-room at Mugby Junction, in the height of the twenty-seven cross draughts (I've often counted 'em while they brush the First-Class hair twenty-seven ways), behind the bottles, among the glasses, bounded on the nor'-west by the beer, stood pretty far to the right of a metallic object that's at times the tea-urn and at times the soup-tureen, according to the nature of the last twang imparted to its contents which are the same groundwork, fended off from the traveller by a barrier of stale sponge-cakes erected atop of the counter, and lastly exposed sideways to the glare of Our Missis's eye – you ask a Boy so situated, next time you stop in a hurry at Mugby, for anything to drink; you take particular notice that he'll try to seem not to hear you, that he'll appear in an absent manner to survey the Line through a transparent medium composed of your head and body, and that he won't serve you as long as you can possibly bear it. *That's* me," he cried exultantly.

The first public Readings of *Barbox Brothers* and *The Boy at Mugby* were given at the St. James's Hall on Tuesday, 15 January, 1867. They were received cordially enough, but it was obvious that they would never rank with the other Readings. Dickens himself was conscious of this and had the two Readings not already been advertised for some of the towns he would have shelved them there and then. As it was they were given four performances before they were taken out of the repertoire.

The first town on the tour was Liverpool, where, he reported to Wills, he did "exactly one million one hundred thousand and one new things with Marigold, which the audience seized each with exactly one million one hundred thousand and one rounds". The weather was bitterly cold and the whole country was frozen up. In Chester he read in a snow storm. He told Mamie: "The hall is like a Methodist chapel in low spirits, and with a cold in its head.

A few blue people shiver at the corners of the street." At Wolverhampton the thaw had set in and it rained heavily. He told Forster: "I am very tired and cannot sleep; have been severely shaken on an atrocious railway." From Leeds he told Mamie: "This is a beastly place with a very good hotel. Except Preston, it is one of the nastiest places I know. The room is like a capacious coal cellar and is indescribably filthy." From Liverpool he told Georgina: "I am not quite right, but believe it to be the effect of the railway shaking. There is no doubt of the fact that, after the Staplehurst experience, it tells more and more, instead of (as one might have expected) less and less." The closing night at Manchester was a great occasion. From Glasgow, which was his next stop, he told Mamie about it: "They cheered me to that extent after it was over, that I was obliged to huddle on my clothes (for I was dressing to prepare for the journey), and go back again. After so heavy a week it *was* rather stiff to start on this long journey at a quarter to two in the morning; but I got more sleep than I ever got in a railway carriage before, and it really was not tedious. The travelling was admirable and a wonderful contrast to my former friend the Midland. I am not by any means knocked up, though I have, as I had on the last series of Readings, a curious feeling of soreness all round the body, which I suppose to arise from the great exertion of voice."

During the tour he often complained of tiredness. The itinerary involved him in rapid and repeated change of nights in distant towns. Nearly every week he was in London for a Reading at the St. James's Hall and on the following morning he was on his way to some provincial town. Day after day he seemed to be doing the same thing at the same time – packing his portmanteau, travelling to a fresh town, unpacking his portmanteau, dining, resting for an hour or so, then making for the hall where his public awaited him. He was unnerved by the amount of travelling on express trains and he asked Dolby to arrange, wherever practicable, to travel by slow ones. Although this dispelled his terror to a great extent it had to be given up, for the delays and monotonies of these journeys were almost as wearing on his nerves as the shaking of the expresses. He was distressed by an inability to sleep and was rapidly becoming exhausted, yet during the closing weeks of the tour, he was discussing with Dolby the prospects of reading in the autumn and winter months. And the great point at issue was whether this tour should be in Britain or America.

PART THREE

The American Tour 1867–68

I begin to feel myself drawn towards America, as Darnay in the Tale of Two Cities was attracted to the Loadstone Rock, Paris.

CHARLES DICKENS to GEORGINA HOGARTH

6

THE SECOND COMING OF DICKENS

DICKENS HAD BEEN receiving offers from America since he first began reading professionally. As far back as January 1859, after the first provincial tour, he had considered an offer from Thomas C. Evans, of New York, who had been deputed by a body of American publishers to negotiate with him. But the terms proposed were too much in the nature of a speculation for Dickens's liking and the negotiations were abandoned. After the Civil War, James T. Fields, his American publisher, raised the subject again and again. Every mail brought Dickens offers from America and every American speculator who came to London went straight to Dolby with similar proposals. Chappells also had asked to undertake the American tour in the event of his going there.

Dickens did not intend to accept any of these offers. He did not believe that anyone in America appreciated the value of the Readings sufficiently to offer him a sum that would make it worth his while. He had made up his mind that if he went at all, he would go on his own account, taking Dolby with him as his manager. He told Forster: "Have no fear that anything will induce me to make the experiment, if I do not see the most forcible reasons for believing that what I could get by it, added to what I have got, would leave me a sufficient fortune." He told Georgina that it was this hope of earning there a large sum of money that drew him towards America "as Darnay in the Tale of Two Cities was attracted to the Loadstone Rock, Paris".

He had reason to be confident that he would make a lot of money in America: all the offers he was receiving pointed to this. But to make absolutely certain, he made inquiries of every likely person. At the end of May 1867 he was still undecided. He told Forster: "I am in a tempest-tossed condition, and can hardly believe that I stand at bay at last on the American question. The difficulty of determining amid the variety of statements made to me is enormous, and you have no idea how the anxiety of it sits upon my soul. But the prize looks so large!"

He knew he must make up his mind quickly. The Presidential election would be held in the autumn of the following year and this would preoccupy the nation, while at the present time everyone in America seemed eager to hear him and their interest was sustained by the strong rumour that he was going there. Early in June he told Fields: "I am trying hard to free myself as to be able to come over and read this next winter. Whether I may succeed in this endeavour or no I cannot yet say, but I am trying HARD. So in the meantime don't contradict the rumour. In the course of the next few mails I hope to be able to give you positive and definite information on the subject."

He decided to settle the question once and for all by sending Dolby to America to report on the prospects. If the visit were found to be impracticable for this year, then he would dismiss the idea from his mind for ever. Chappells had agreed to let him have the services of Dolby for the duration of the American enterprise. On 13 June Dickens told Fields: "I have this morning resolved to send out to Boston in the first week of August, Mr. Dolby, the secretary and manager of my Readings. He is profoundly versed in the business of these delightful intellectual feasts(?) and will come straight to Ticknor and Fields and hold solemn council with them, and will then go to New York, Philadelphia, Hartford, Washington, etc., and see the rooms for himself and make his estimates. He will then telegraph to me, 'I see my way to such and such results; shall I go on?' If I reply 'Yes', I shall stand committed to begin reading in America with the month of December. If I reply 'No', it will be because I do not clearly see the game to be worth so large a candle."

There was a further matter on which Dickens was anxious to have Dolby's report. Twenty-four years had elapsed since the burning of *Martin Chuzzlewit* in New York, but he wanted to know if any residue of bitterness and ill-will still remained. His American friends had assured him that he had nothing to fear, but he could not help feeling a little apprehensive. The rowdy press might still cherish a grudge against him and make his second visit to America the occasion to resurrect the quarrels that had broken out after his first.

When Dickens first set foot on American soil in 1842 it would have seemed unthinkable both to himself and the thousands of Americans who cheered him that the visit was to result in acrimony. His name was as well known in America as it was in Britain and he was given a tremendous reception. Never since Lafayette had a foreigner received such a welcome. Dickens had come in the friendliest spirit, ready to admire everything. He was sympathetic to the United States as a democratic, kingless country, freed from class rule. As a radical he believed that Britain had much to learn from America. But the more he saw of the country the more uneasy he became. There was not the abolition of poverty he had expected to find; the running of schools, workhouses and prisons was no more enlightened than in Britain; and he found in the corruption of the politicians, the rowdiness of the press and the horrors of slavery evils he had never before encountered. He was disgusted by the philistinism, the lack of refinement, the boastfulness, the passion for making money and the love of smart dealing. He told Macready: "This is not the republic I came to see, this is not the republic of my imagination."

In *American Notes*, published in 1842, Dickens praised many of the things he had seen, but his admiration was outweighed by his criticism. The book caused great offence in America. The rowdy press attacked Dickens for daring to find fault with the country. The rowdy press had no counterpart in Britain, where newspapers were read chiefly by the middle and upper classes. In America the newspaper was the staple reading of the great majority of the people and to attract readers editors vied with one another in sensationalism. Their main weapon was the libellous personal attack and they spared no one from the President downwards. Of all the rowdy newspapers, James Gordon Bennett's *New York Herald* was the rowdiest. Bennett declared that Dickens had "the most coarse, vulgar, impudent and superficial mind" ever to write about "this original and remarkable country".

The Americans had a further reason for being angry with Dickens. It seemed to them terribly ungrateful that he should have written an unfriendly book after having received so great a welcome. This attitude puzzled him. He could not understand why the Americans should have expected him, who had criticised his own country so much, not to criticise theirs. He had said much harder things about Britain than he had said about America. Such intolerance of criticism angered him and resulted in the American chapters of *Martin Chuzzlewit*, published the following year. In

June 1843, when Dickens decided to send Martin to America, he was still being calumnied in the rowdy press and every mail-boat from America brought him abusive letters. He was disgusted with the country and in *Martin Chuzzlewit* he intended to give "the eagle a final poke under the fifth rib".

For Americans, reading *Martin Chuzzlewit* had the quality of a nightmare. All the faults of national character were paraded before them. Nowhere in the book was there a mention of the virtues described in *American Notes*. Dickens, writing at the height of his powers, held up a mirror to the vulgar, boastful, philistine, smart-dealing America of the eighteen-forties, the land of the almighty dollar. The book aroused the Americans to a fury. Thomas Carlyle wrote: "All Yankee-Doodle-dum blazed up like one universal soda bottle." Feeling against Dickens ran so high that he dared not travel to Liverpool to say goodbye to Macready, when the actor set sail for a tour of the United States. He feared his presence on the dock would be fatal to Macready's success.

But America had changed since then. The old controversy aroused little animosity in a generation matured by the most terrible civil war in the history of mankind. Dickens was reassured by an article which appeared in the *New York Times* while Dolby was in America on his tour of inspection. The *Times* declared: "Even in England Dickens is less well-known than here, and of the millions here who cherish every word he has written, there are tens of thousands who would make a large sacrifice to see and hear the man who has made happy so many homes. Whatever sensitiveness there once was to sneering criticism, the lapse of a quarter of a century, and the profound significance of a great war, have modified or removed."

On his arrival in Boston Dolby was met by James T. Fields, Howard Ticknor and James R. Osgood of the firm of Ticknor and Fields, publishers of the only authorised American editions of Dickens's works. He had been instructed by Dickens to act in conjunction with the firm and Osgood was assigned to accompany him on his tour of inspection. Before leaving Boston Dolby sought the opinions of literary men, among them Emerson, Holmes and Longfellow. Emerson and Holmes had no doubt of the success of the Readings as far as Boston was concerned, while Longfellow admonished him not to dare to return to America without Dickens.

In New York Dolby consulted the newspaper editors. Horace Greeley of the *Tribune* believed that financially the visit of Dickens would eclipse that of Jenny Lind. He wrote in a leading article: "The fame as a novelist which Mr. Dickens has already created in America, and which at the *best* has never yielded him anything particularly munificent or substantial, is become his capital stock in the present enterprise." William Cullen Bryant of the *Evening Post* was equally enthusiastic. Dickens's old enemy, James Gordon Bennett of the *Herald*, was most interested in "the second coming of Dickens", as he termed it. He declared that if Dickens would first apologise to the American people for *Martin Chuzzlewit* and *American Notes*, he would make a lot of money. Dolby promised to pass on this opinion, together with Bennett's advice "not to charge less than ten dollars to see and hear Dickens". The next morning, just to stir things up a little, Bennett presented his readers with a reprint of *American Notes* as a "special", free of cost, but the current generation was untroubled by the book.

While in New York Dolby consulted several showmen, foremost among them Phineas Taylor Barnum, who assured him that the Readings would be a sensational success. Barnum's opinion was endorsed by Harry Palmer of Niblo's Gardens and Lafayette Harrison of the Irving Hall. Dolby then travelled to Washington, and as the views expressed there were the same as those of Boston and New York, he saw no reason to pursue his inquiries further and he sailed for Britain on 11 September.

On his return he submitted to Dickens a lengthy report, including plans of various halls, calculations of expenses and prices of admission. Dickens condensed this to a short document entitled "The Case in a Nutshell", which concluded that a series of eighty Readings, comprised within six months, would yield a clear profit of £15,500, even allowing seven dollars to the pound on converting American paper money into gold.

Forster disagreed violently with every statement in "The Case in a Nutshell". Throughout all the discussions of the American trip he had tried steadily to dissuade Dickens from going, not only because he believed, as always, that reading was an unworthy employment for a man of Dickens's genius but also because he did not think Dickens was in a fit state to undertake such an arduous tour. His fears were well-founded. While Dolby was in America, Dickens had been ill. He was laid up with another attack in his foot and the pain was so great that he could not bear to have the fomentations taken off for a moment. Sir Henry Thompson had diagnosed gout, but Dickens persisted in his belief that the condition was only a local one. He told Forster: "I make out so many reasons against supposing it to be gouty, that I really do not think it is."

Forster was so anxious that Dickens should not endanger his health by going to America that he brought out every argument against the enterprise that he could think of, no matter how unreasonable. He told Dolby that ever since the Staplehurst accident Dickens had been in bad health and that a sea voyage was the very worst thing for him. If he went there would be a recurrence of the Forrest-Macready riots, as all America knew of the friendship between Dickens and Macready. He was certain there was no money in America, and even if there were, Dickens would not get any of it; and even if he did, the Irish and the book-sellers would break into his hotel and rob him; and even if he deposited his money in a bank, the bank would surely fail. He believed that the calculation of £15,500 in eighty Readings was all nonsense, as the halls were not large enough and even if they were, there were not enough people in America to fill them.

But Forster's opinions failed to carry the day and on 30 September the word "Yes" was cabled to Ticknor and Fields. Dolby sailed again for America on 12 October. Dickens was to follow him on 9 November. On 2 November a farewell dinner was given in Dickens's honour at the Freemasons' Hall. It was a brilliant occasion, with four hundred and fifty guests led by the Lord Mayor of London and the Lord Chief Justice. The chairman was Lord Lytton and in his speech he said: "Happy is the man who makes clear his title deeds to the royalty of genius while he yet lives to enjoy the gratitude and reverence of those he has subjected to his sway. . . . Seldom has that kind of royalty been quietly conceded to any man of genius until his tomb becomes his throne and yet there is not one of us now present who thinks it strange that it is granted without a murmur to the guest whom we receive tonight."

Dickens was given a great ovation and the tears streamed down his cheeks. When he recovered from his emotion he made an eloquent speech, in the course of which he referred to his forthcoming visit to America and affirmed his faith in the American people: "I know full well, whatever little motes my beamy eyes may have decried in theirs, that they are a kind, large-hearted, generous and great people. In that faith I am going to see them again: in that faith I shall, please God, return from them in the spring; in that same faith to live and die."

Outside the hall a great crowd of ordinary people was waiting to say goodbye to him. When he appeared a very old woman came forward and kissed his hand. As he stood there, looking down on her bowed head, his face was pale. On 8 November, another mark of esteem was shown him when he was conveyed to Liverpool in a royal saloon carriage. The following morning he sailed aboard the *Cuba* for America.

Dolby had arrived in Boston to find the city agog at the prospect of Dickens's visit. Tongue in cheek, the *New York Tribune* reported: "No sooner was the news flashed along the cable, that he was coming, than everything was immediately put in apple-pie order. The streets were all swept from one end of the city to the other for the second time in twenty-four hours. The State House and the Old South Church were painted, off hand, a delicate rose pink." On the receipt of the cable, Ticknor and Fields had gone ahead with the arrangements for the tour. The price of admission had not yet been fixed and, after much discussion, it was decided to charge two dollars a ticket, the price to include a reserved seat. A difficulty arose over the printing of the bills and posters. Dickens always used an orange-coloured paper. This was his favourite colour. He had used it for all advertisements for his books since *Pickwick Papers* and for all publicity connected with the Readings. Dolby was aware that Dickens wanted the American Readings to be identical in every respect with the British, but paper of this colour seemed to be unobtainable in the United States. Eventually a supply was located and two tons ordered. As it turned out, such a large quantity was unnecessary. After the first series of Readings in Boston and New York, not a bill or poster was printed for the whole of the American tour.

The excitement in Boston over Dickens's visit increased when it was announced that the first Reading of the American tour would take place there on 2 December, 1867. It was also announced that the sale of tickets for the first four Boston Readings would be held at the publishing house of Ticknor and Fields on Monday, 18 November, two days before Dickens's expected arrival. Dolby feared that the general public would have little chance of buying tickets, for he had heard that, in addition to the Boston speculators, others were arriving from New York. The aim of the speculators was to buy up as many tickets as possible in order to sell them over again at a profit. Already he was receiving letters from persons who were all apparently blind, crippled or paralysed. All the writers were unable to queue for tickets and all of them wanted front seats.

On the evening before the sale a man burst into Dolby's bedroom moaning pitifully. He told Dolby that from childhood he had suffered from pains in his back and dared not risk exposure to the cold night air. It would be inhuman to expect him to stand in the queue and he would consider it a great convenience if Dolby could let him have his tickets there and then. He had a large family and needed a dozen tickets for each Reading, more if they could be spared. When his request was refused, he left the room and Dolby heard his cries of pain dying away down the corridor. An hour later he saw the invalid in the hotel bar. He seemed in perfect health and spirits, and he invited Dolby to have a drink with him. He was one of the advance guard of speculators from New York and next morning he was among the first in the queue.

The queue began to form at seven-thirty on Sunday evening. The temperature was below freezing point. By ten o'clock there were fifty people in the queue. Some had brought armchairs, others had mattresses and blankets, and stretched themselves out on the pavement. By midnight there were a hundred people in the queue which grew steadily hour by hour. They stamped their feet to keep warm and sang boisterous songs to pass the time. Friends relieved friends. Some were obliged to drop from the line through sheer exhaustion, others through having drunk too much. One man, true to the American tradition, thought the occasion warranted an oration. He addressed the queue: "Gentlemen, there are but three men who have stamped themselves upon the civilization of the nineteenth century. Those men, gentlemen, are Charles Shakespeare, William Dickens and – myself." At this point he was too overcome, either by emotion or bourbon, to continue.

By eight o'clock in the morning the queue was half-a-mile long. Kate Field, the Boston journalist, reported: "So closely packed was the human file as to seem as if the living mass had been caught and skewered for some special cannibalistic festival, preparatory to being roasted on a spit." Standing in the queue were "truckmen, porters, clerks, 'roughs', clergymen, merchants, gamblers, speculators, gentlemen, loafers, white men, black men, coloured men, boys and *three* women! Broadcloth, no cloth! Fine linen, doubtful linen, no linen! The lion stood up with the lamb."

A stranger arriving from out of town asked a bystander the cause of so large and excited a gathering. " 'T'ain't election-time down here, is it?"

"Oh no, we're buying tickets, sir."

"Buying tickets? – for what?"

"For Dickens's Readings."

"Dickens! Who the devil is Dickens?"

"Why, don't you know? – The great novelist."

"Never heard of him in all my born days, but if there is any critter on earth that can keep such a crowd together with the mercury clear way out of sight, damned if I don't see him!"

The sale commenced at nine o'clock and lasted eleven hours until every ticket for the first four Readings was sold. The receipts totalled fourteen thousand dollars, which, allowing for depreciation in converting American paper money into gold, came to two thousand pounds. While the sale was in progress a telegram from Halifax was handed to Dolby, announcing the arrival of the *Cuba*, *en route* for Boston, with Dickens on board. When Dolby read the telegram to the crowd they went wild with delight. The news enhanced the value of the tickets and the speculators did a roaring trade. Two dollar tickets in a good position near the platform were immediately bought for as much as twenty-six dollars each.

Great crowds began assembling at Boston Harbour on 19 November to greet Dickens when he landed. Dolby, however, was anxious to save his Chief the strain of a reception after the fatigue of a long voyage, so he steamed down in a Customs-House boat to pick Dickens up before the *Cuba* docked. Dickens's cheery voice greeted him from the deck of the *Cuba*. He had already heard from the pilot, twenty miles out, the result of the ticket sale. He regarded this as a great compliment from the Bostonians, as very few had heard him read and had little idea of what the Readings were like. They landed quietly at Long Wharf, where a carriage was waiting to take them to the Parker House Hotel. In half-an-hour Dickens was sitting down to dinner, quite prepared, as he said, to give the first Reading that very night, if necessary.

But twelve days had to elapse before the first Reading and he

Dickens as Fagin in *Sikes and Nancy* (*Tinsleys' Magazine*)

Dickens as Nancy in *Sikes and Nancy* (*Tinsleys' Magazine*)

chafed against the delay. He passed the time rehearsing and going for long walks in Boston and the neighbourhood. He found that the city had grown enormously in twenty-five years and become more mercantile. He told Mamie that it looked "like Leeds mixed with Preston, and flavoured with New Brighton; but for smoke and fog you substitute an exquisitely bright light air". He was pleased to notice that the people in the streets behaved with reserve towards him. He told Georgina: "The Bostonians having been duly informed that I wish to be quiet, really leave me as much as I should be in Manchester and Liverpool. This I cannot expect to last elsewhere; but it is a most welcome relief here, as I have all the Readings to get up. The people are perfectly kind and perfectly agreeable. If I stop to look in at a shop-window, a score of passers-by stop; and after I begin to read, I cannot expect in the natural course of things to get off so easily. But I every day take from seven to ten miles in peace."

He received many invitations, but, with the exception of those from Fields and Longfellow, all were refused. Longfellow was now white-haired, white-bearded, but remarkably handsome, still living in his old house, where his beautiful wife was burnt to death. Dickens told Charley: "I dined with him the other day, and could not get the terrific scene out of my imagination. She was in a blaze in an instant, rushed into his arms with a wild cry and never spoke afterwards." Already there were complaints about the limitations of the tour. Five hundred undergraduates at Cambridge, unable to obtain tickets for the Readings, had asked Longfellow to intercede with Dickens on their behalf. Letters were arriving from towns in all parts of the country begging him to come and read. "I don't know what is to be done," Dickens told Georgina despairingly.

He was anxious to start work, "for I yearn to begin to check the Readings off", he told Wills, "and feel myself tending towards home". He was missing Ellen Ternan. Up to the moment of sailing he had hoped that she too might come to America. He had even delayed his decision on this until he reached Boston, in case he should think of some way that would make it possible for her to join him. Before he left Britain he had instructed Wills: "On the day after my arrival out I will send you a short telegram at the office. Please copy its exact words (as they will have a special meaning for her) and post them to her as above by the very next post after receiving my telegram."

On 22 November, three days after Dickens's arrival in Boston, Wills received a telegram which read: "Safe and well expect good letter full of hope." The special meaning of this for Ellen only became clear in the following century when in Dickens's small pocket diary for 1867 this code was found:

> Tel: all well means *you come*
>
> Tel: safe and well means *you don't come*

So Ellen was not to join him. He had realised that, in the glare of publicity which would surround him wherever he went in America, it would be impossible for her to be with him.

Two days after Dickens's arrival in Boston Dolby and Osgood left for New York, where the sale of tickets for the first four Readings there was to be held on 29 November. They expected trouble, for they had heard that the speculators were to be out in force. Already someone in New York was forging tickets for the Readings, which meant that each ticket would now have to be over-printed with a special stamp. The night before the sale the queue began to form outside the Steinway Hall, where the Readings were to take place. The crowd passed the time singing, dancing, drinking and indulging in occasional fights. It reminded Dolby of the night before a public execution. By morning there were at least five thousand people in the queue. Men offered ten to twenty dollars for a place near the head of the line. Waiters flew across the streets and squares to serve breakfast in the open air.

The sale was to start at nine o'clock and at eight o'clock Dolby and Osgood, accompanied by Harry Palmer and the police captain of the local precinct, inspected the queue. In Palmer's opinion, forty-five out of the first fifty men were certainly speculators. Dolby was anxious to thwart their plans and he asked Palmer for his advice, thinking that Palmer, as the owner of Niblo's Gardens, must be very knowledgeable about the ways of the speculators. Palmer had noticed that nearly all the speculators in the queue were wearing caps and he suggested to Dolby that tickets be sold only to men in hats. Dolby thought this a little rough on men who had been standing out in the cold all night, but he wanted to give the public a fair chance and he agreed to Palmer's suggestion.

When the ticket-office opened and the police passed word down the queue that tickets would be sold only to people in hats, there was great consternation, not only among the speculators but also among those members of the public who happened to be wearing caps. The speculators proved equal to the situation. Within seconds hats had been collected from waiters in neighbouring restaurants and elsewhere. By changing caps for hats at the entrance, the speculators gained possession of most of the first seven or eight rows in the hall. Two hours after the sale had commenced they were already selling the best seats at enormous profits.

Dolby arrived back in Boston, in readiness for the first Reading there, to find himself the most abused man in America, especially in Bennett's *New York Herald*, while the New York *World* remarked: "Surely it is time that the pudding-headed Dolby retired into the native gloom from which he has emerged." This marked the beginning of the anger of the general public over the speculators' success. Dickens was shocked at the tone of the newspapers. He feared that the speculators would prejudice the success of the tour.

The first American Reading took place at the Tremont Temple in Boston on Monday, 2 December, 1867. The hall, which held two thousand people, had a raked floor and excellent acoustics. Every local notability was present. Reporters had come from New York and columns of description were printed in the New York as well as in the Boston newspapers. When Dickens appeared on the platform his reception was as great as at Manchester and Edinburgh. Then there was a deep silence as he prepared to read. The programme was the *Carol* and the *Pickwick Trial*. At the end of the *Carol* a sigh came from the audience followed by cheers and shouts, so enthusiastic and uproarious, that he broke his rule and came on the platform again to bow his acknowledgments. After a ten-minute break he read the *Pickwick Trial*. Stimulated by the audience he indulged in so many ad-libs that it seemed to Dolby that the Reading might almost be regarded as a new edition from the author.

The next day Dickens told Forster: "It is really impossible to exaggerate the magnificence of the reception or the effect of the Reading. The whole city will talk of nothing else and hear of nothing else today." *Copperfield* went well that night, although he had the impression that it was "a thought too delicate" for the Bostonians. At all the Boston Readings there were shorthand writers sent by pirate publishers to take down every word, but Ticknor and Fields spoiled these plans by quickly issuing cheap editions of the Readings.

As in Britain the plan was to give four Readings each week on Monday, Tuesday, Thursday and Friday, leaving three days for rest or travel. Invitations for Dickens to read were still pouring in from all parts of the States, but he now realised that it would be impossible to satisfy these demands and he had no intention of extending the tour. Moreover, he had learnt that Doctor Hayes, the arctic explorer, had forecast a very severe winter and travelling conditions were likely to be difficult. This forecast, together with the success of the Boston Readings and the prospect of a similar success in New York, justified him in cutting down the tour list. He had intended to read in Canada and Nova Scotia before re-embarking for Britain, but now he decided to go no farther north than Portland, taking in the New England States *en route* and until the early part of January the Readings were to be confined to Boston and New York.

Dickens, accompanied by Dolby, left Boston for New York on

7 December. With two ferry crossings at Stonington and New London, the journey took nine hours. Travelling by rail in America was not very comfortable. Sometimes Dickens was able to enjoy the privacy of a "drawing-room" car, but more often he travelled in a long car built to carry fifty-two passengers, with double seats on either side of a broad gangway. At each end of the car was a stove, which was kept red hot during the winter months and made the atmosphere inside the car unbearably stuffy. But at least he was spared the high speeds of the British expresses and his journeys in America did much to allay his dread of railway travelling.

When he arrived in New York he was tired and feverish. He had caught a cold in Boston and during the railway journey it had turned catarrhal. Dolby had reserved a suite of apartments for him at the Westminster Hotel, owned by Harry Palmer. It was a quiet hotel. The waiters were French and he felt as if he were living in Paris. He was pleased with the arrangements made for his comfort. Palmer had detailed a boy to be in constant attendance outside his sitting-room to prevent intrusions on his privacy and had also arranged for him to have the exclusive use of a private stairway, so that he could come and go without being seen by the public.

The next day he went sightseeing in New York. Dolby had hired a very smart carriage "and", Dickens told Mamie, "if you were to behold me driving out, furred up to the moustache, with furs on the coach bay and on the driver, and with an immense white, red, and yellow striped rug for a covering, you would suppose me to be of Hungarian or Polish nationality". The city had changed so much in twenty-five years that he had difficulty in finding a familiar landmark. He told Wills: "The place has grown out of my knowledge, and is enormous. Everything in it looks as if the order of nature was reversed, and everything grows newer every day instead of older."

Every window in Broadway seemed to be displaying his portrait and every theatre seemed to be playing one of his works.

He did not visit any theatres while in New York with the exception of Niblo's Gardens, where he saw *The Black Crook*. This great spectacle had been running for sixteen months and was making a fortune for Harry Palmer. He told Forster: "The people who act in it have not the slightest idea of what it is about, and never had; but, after taxing my intellectual powers to the utmost, I fancy I have discovered Black Crook to be a malignant hunchback leagued with the Powers of Darkness to separate two lovers; and that the Powers of Lightness coming (in no skirts whatever) to the rescue, he is defeated. I am quite serious in saying that I do not suppose there are two pages of *All the Year Round* in the whole piece (which acts all night); the whole of the rest of it being ballets of all sorts, perfectly unaccountable processions, and the Donkey out of last year's Covent Garden pantomime!"

The first New York Reading took place on Monday, 9 December. Kate Field described the scene in front of the Steinway Hall: "Carriage after carriage deposited its burden on the sidewalk, while a throng of men and boys, who may be called the 'outs', choked up the passage-way and gazed at the fortunate possessors of tickets with about the same expression as that with which hungry children eye the contents of pastry-cooks' windows. Speculators to right of us, speculators to left of us, speculators in front of us volleyed and thundered. The very best seats in the house were held by these vampires. They knew it, and great was the profit thereof; for it would have cost some people a great deal more – in feelings – to have remained away than to have paid ten or twenty dollars for a ticket. An American public is not to be held in check by gigantic swindling; hence the breed of vampires."

The scene in the foyer was equally animated: "Everybody was on the *qui vive* to see who had been shrewd enough to secure seats, and apparently seemed astonished that anybody had been as clever as himself. The salutation between friends was not the ordinary 'How are you?' but, for this night only, 'Where did you get your ticket?' Then followed a thrilling narration of hair-breadth 'scapes, listened to with breathless attention."

The New York Readings were a triumph for Dickens. He did not think it possible to have a more brilliant success. He told Georgina: "They are a wonderfully fine audience, even better than Edinburgh, and almost, if not quite as good as Paris." "Amazing success," he told Mamie. "A very fine audience, far better than at Boston. Carol and Trial on first night, great: still greater Copperfield and Bob on second." By the end of the week he was feeling the exertion of reading with a heavy cold in the enormous Steinway Hall.

He was as well-known in the streets of New York as he was in London. He told Forster: "People will turn back, turn again and face me, and have a look at me, or will say to one another, 'Look here! Dickens coming!' But no one ever stops me or addresses me. Sitting reading in the carriage outside the New York post-office while one of the staff was stamping letters inside, I became conscious that a few people who had been looking at the turn-out had discovered me within. On my peeping out good-humouredly, one of them (I should say a merchant's book-keeper) stepped up to the door, took off his hat, and said in a frank way: 'Mr. Dickens, I should very much like to have the honour of shaking hands with you' – and, that done, presented two others. Nothing could be more quiet or less intrusive." This respect for his privacy shown in every city on this second visit was in marked contrast to the insolent prying which had annoyed him so much on the first.

The sale of tickets for the next four New York Readings, which were to take place the following week, was held on Wednesday, 11 December. The weather was bitterly cold, with all the signs that a fall of snow was imminent, but this did not stop people from queuing all night. By the time the ticket-office opened the queue was three-quarters of a mile long. In a desperate attempt to keep the best tickets out of the hands of the specula-tors, Dolby ordered the clerks to commence selling at the tenth row of seats and then after selling to the first fifty in the queue to start selling at the first row. By this means he hoped that the general public would get a chance of the best seats. The speculators were incensed and accused him of infringing their democratic rights. Especially voluble on this issue was one old speculator, dressed appropriately as George Washington in wig, three-cornered hat, cut-away coat and knee-breeches.

Also among the first in the queue were two young city clerks, who found themselves supplied with tickets for the back of the hall. One of them went straight to the police and took out a summons against Dickens for obtaining money under false pretences. That evening, while Dickens was at dinner, the summons was served personally by the Marshall, who was so astonished at finding himself in the same room as Dickens and also by Dickens's pleasant invitation to join him in a glass of champagne that he was completely overcome. He drank his wine too quickly and had to be led, coughing and spluttering, from the room. When the clerk's employers heard of his action he was instantly dismissed, but Dickens interceded with them on his behalf and, after the young man had withdrawn his action, he was re-instated.

After the sale of tickets Dickens ranked Dolby as "the most unpopular and best-abused man in America." He told Forster: "He cannot get four thousand people into a room holding only two thousand, he cannot induce people to pay at the ordinary price for themselves, instead of giving thrice as much to speculators, and he is attacked in all directions." Dolby could not beat the speculators. He allowed no more than six tickets to any one person for a course of four Readings, but the speculators employed large numbers of men to buy for them. One of the biggest could put fifty men in a queue at any time and so get three hundred tickets into his own hands. This particular speculator stayed in the same hotels as Dickens and Dolby so that he could watch their movements. The public could have done away with the abuse by refusing to buy from the speculators at increased prices, but the great mass of people found it preferable to pay five to ten dollars for a two-dollar ticket than to stand all night in a queue, and so the speculator prospered.

On the evening of the sale the expected snow had begun to fall and by the following afternoon the streets were covered to a depth of eighteen inches. This was the start of the severe weather, which was to last almost up to the very end of the tour. The New Yorkers quickly adapted themselves to the new conditions. Every vehicle which had previously been running on wheels was transformed as if by magic into a sleigh. Not a wheel, except on the tramcars, was to be seen in the city. Dickens hired an elegant sleigh and that weekend enjoyed some exhilarating drives. "Everybody sleighing," he told Wills. "Everybody coming to the Readings. There were at least ten thousand sleighs in the Park last Sunday. Your illustrious chief – in a red sleigh covered with furs, and drawn by a pair of fine horses covered with bells, and tearing up 14 miles of snow an hour – made an imposing appearance." But during the second week in New York his cold became so bad that he was confined to the hotel, only going out in the evening to read. His heart was also troubling him. After the Reading on Monday night he had to be helped to bed in a very faint condition and the following morning he was not able to get up until noon.

Four days later, on Saturday, 21 December, Dickens and Dolby left New York for Boston. They travelled on the mid-day train, so that Dickens would not be hurried in the morning, for his cold was causing him sleepless nights. He told Mamie: "It is a bad country to be unwell and travelling in; you are one of say a hundred people in a heated car, with a great stove in it, and all the little windows closed, and the hurrying and banging about are indescribable. The atmosphere is detestable and the motion often all but intolerable." The speculators had left before them. After selling their tickets for the New York Readings, they had travelled to Boston for the sale of tickets for the two Christmas Readings to be given in the city.

By this time four Readings had been given in Boston and eight in New York. Their success had proved that there was no need to take in smaller cities on the tour except to break long journeys. Osgood, having the best knowledge of the country, was asked to plan a new tour. This was a good time to do it, as the only place Dickens was pledged to visit was Philadelphia for eight Readings, in four visits of two Readings each.

Dolby's original plan was to read at least once a week in New York, but Dickens was against this. He argued that by 10 January he would have read to thirty-five thousand people in New York and therefore it would be wiser not to read there again for some time in case the people tired of him. He told Dolby: "It is one of the popular peculiarities which I most particularly notice, that they must not have a thing too easily. Nothing in the country lasts long; and a thing is prized the more the less easy it is made." It was decided, therefore, to close up in New York in the middle of January and not go there again except for five farewell Readings in April. Boston was to be treated in the same way, with the exception of one visit in the last week in February for four Readings.

The tour was to be confined chiefly to the eastern seaboard States and was designed to induce the public to come to Dickens rather than he should go to them. In addition to Boston, New York and Philadelphia, the towns included were: Brooklyn, Baltimore, Washington, Cincinnati, Chicago, St. Louis, Hartford, Providence, Syracuse, Rochester, Buffalo, Albany, Springfield, Worcester, New Bedford and Portland. Buffalo was included because Dickens planned a pleasure trip to Niagara and Buffalo was *en route*. As things turned out, the Readings in Cincinnati, Chicago and St. Louis were never given.

The two Christmas Readings at Boston were emotional occasions, especially the Reading of the *Carol* on Christmas Eve. Dickens's catarrh was dragging him down and it was as much as he could do to get through the Readings. Fields had feared that they might have to be cancelled, but Dickens told him that no man had a right to break an engagement with the public if he were able to be out of bed. Christmas Day, 1867, was a miserable one for Dickens. On that day he left Boston for New York, where he was scheduled to give five Readings, commencing the following night. He was depressed not only at leaving his friends on such a day but also at the prospect of the long train journey. Two days later he was so ill that Dr. Fordyce Barker was called in. Barker diagnosed nervous exhaustion and an irritated condition of the uvula. He told Dickens that he might have to stop reading for a while. Dickens had no intention of giving in and he instructed Dolby to continue with the arrangements for the next stage of the tour.

Dolby found it necessary to increase his staff of clerks, for in the next few weeks he had to prepare for sale nine thousand tickets for Philadelphia, eight thousand for Brooklyn, eight thousand for Baltimore and six thousand for Washington. To frustrate the plans of the speculators, he had decided to superintend personally the sale of tickets in each city. This meant that he would travel ahead of Dickens, although he would try as far as possible to be occasionally present at the Readings. These arrangements were approved by Dickens, but he dreaded losing Dolby's company. Dickens was cheered by the news from London of the success of the dramatised version of *No Thoroughfare* at the Adelphi Theatre, with his friend Charles Fechter in the leading role. The Swiss Mountain Pass scene, which he himself had designed with the scene painter, had been highly praised.

On 2 January, 1868, he read *Doctor Marigold* at the Steinway Hall for the first time in America. It made a tremendous hit. At the end the audience gave a shout of delight and rushed towards the platform as if they were going to carry him off. He was becoming aware of American preferences in the Readings. *Boots* and *Nickleby* were extraordinarily successful in both New York and Boston, whereas the New Yorkers appreciated *Copperfield* more than the Bostonians. The great favourites in both cities were the *Carol* and the *Pickwick Trial*, and this proved to be the case in the other fifteen cities visited on the American tour. Of the nine Readings that comprised the American repertoire, the *Carol* and the *Pickwick Trial* held pride of place. The *Pickwick Trial* was read thirty-five times and the *Carol* twenty-five. *Bob Sawyer's Party* and *Marigold* came next with twenty-one and eighteen Readings respectively. These were followed by *Boots* with fourteen Readings, then *Copperfield* and *Nickleby* with thirteen Readings each. *Little Dombey* was given five Readings and *Mrs. Gamp* four.

Generally Dickens found the Americans were good audiences. He told Fechter: "They do not (I think) perceive touches of art to *be* art; but they are responsive to the bold results of such touches." He thought them more humorous than formerly, "and," he told Forster, "there must be a great deal of innocent imagination among every class, or they never could pet with such extraordinary pleasure as they do, the Boots' story of the elopement of the two little children. They seem to see the children; and the women set up a shrill undercurrent of half-pity and half-pleasure that is quite affecting."

He returned to Boston to give two Readings on 6 and 7 January, then went back to New York to give two Readings on the 9th and 10th. With the last Reading in New York approximately a quarter of the American Readings had been given. After deducting all expenses Dolby remitted ten thousand pounds to London. Dickens reported to Forster: "Well, the work is hard, the climate is hard, the life is hard; but so far the gain is enormous. My cold steadily refuses to stir an inch. It distresses me greatly at times, though it is always good enough to leave me for the needful two hours. I have tried allopathy, homeopathy, cold things, warm things, bitter things, stimulants, narcotics, all with the same result. Nothing will touch it." This was his condition when the New York Readings closed on 10 January. So far the tour had been confined to Boston and New York, but now the hard travelling was about to begin.

7

HARD TRAVELLING

The next stop after New York was Philadelphia. At the first Reading there the audience were so astounded when Dickens simply walked on to the platform and opened his book, that for a moment he wondered what could be the matter. He told Forster: "They evidently thought that there ought to have been a flourish, and Dolby sent on to prepare for me. With them it is the simplicity of the operation that raises wonder. With the newspapers 'Mr. Dickens's extraordinary composure' is not reasoned out as being necessary to the art of the thing, but is sensitively watched with a lurking doubt whether it may not imply disparagement of the audience."

He had sensed the same disappointment in the audiences at Boston and New York over his lack of ostentation. "They are all so accustomed to do public things with a flourish of trumpets, that the notion of my coming in to read without someone first flying up and delivering an 'Oration' about me, and flying down again and leading me in, is so very unaccountable to them, that sometimes they have no idea until I open my lips that it can possibly be Charles Dickens."

In Philadelphia, when the initial astonishment of the audience had passed, he found them very responsive to the *Carol* and the *Pickwick Trial*. The following night, when he read *Copperfield* and *Bob Sawyer's Party*, they were again "ready and bright", but he thought they had understood the *Carol* better than *Copperfield*.

Before the next two Readings at Philadelphia he had to travel back to New York, for four Readings he was scheduled to give at Brooklyn commencing 16 January. In Brooklyn the "noble army of speculators", as he described them, had turned out for the sale of tickets, each man furnished with "a straw mattress, a little bag of bread and meat, two blankets, and a bottle of whisky". They lighted a great bonfire and took turns sleeping round it. This fire was a great danger in a narrow street consisting mainly of wooden houses, and at daybreak the police intervened. While the speculators in the front of the queue were busily engaged fighting off the police, the people farther back rushed forward and claimed the places nearest the door. At Brooklyn the only suitable hall for the Readings was the Plymouth Church and Dickens had already beguiled Forster's imagination with the prospect of these "ecclesiastical entertainments". He told him: "We let the seats pew by pew! the pulpit is taken down for my screen and gas! and I appear out of the vestry in canonical form!"

From Brooklyn he travelled back to Philadelphia. This double crossing fatigued him and did nothing to improve his cold, which, he told Fields, "remains just as it was (beastly) and where it was (in the head)". He had left off referring to the subject "except in emphatic sniffs, convulsive wheezes and resounding sneezes". He did not help matters by his practice, when travelling, of standing on the brake outside the railway car to avoid the heat and stuffiness inside. He would stand there until the snow and the wind and the flying steam drove him inside again.

He was also distressed by sleeplessness and lack of appetite. Sometimes he could get no rest until morning. He rarely took any breakfast. He had a light meal at three o'clock and ate nothing more until after the Reading, when he had another light meal. To sustain him through the Reading he had established the custom of taking an egg beaten up in a glass of sherry before going on to the platform and another between the parts. Because of his poor health, he decided to cut out the distant cities of Chicago, St. Louis and Cincinnati. Dolby had already set off for Chicago to make arrangements for the sale of tickets, but Dickens recalled him to Philadelphia. He told Dolby that they would content themselves with nearer, if smaller, places and thereby get home almost a month earlier. Dickens's decision not to visit Chicago caused great annoyance in that city. George W. Childs, publisher of the Philadelphia *Public Ledger*, told him that if he did not read in Chicago the people would go into fits. Dickens replied that he would rather they went into fits than he did.

After Philadelphia his journey lay southwards, to Baltimore and Washington. The sales of tickets in these towns had passed off quietly, for the New York speculators, reckoning neither place to be worth their while, had stayed away. From Baltimore on 29 January he told Georgina: "This is one of the places where Butler carried it with a high hand during the war, and where the ladies used to spit when they passed a Northern soldier. They are very handsome women, with an Eastern touch in them, and dress brilliantly. They are a bright responsive people likewise and very pleasant to read to."

The Washington Readings were held in the Carroll Hall, a comparatively small building, capable of holding slightly over a thousand people. Because of the limited space Dolby had wanted to charge five dollars a ticket, but Dickens thought this excessive. Dolby had pointed out that, thanks to the speculators, the audiences in Boston, New York, Philadelphia and Brooklyn had all paid an average of five dollars a ticket. On reflection, however, he agreed to reduce the price of the Washington tickets to three dollars. Horace Greeley, of the *New York Tribune*, had advised Dickens not to read in Washington. He told him that it was highly probable that President Andrew Johnson would be impeached. Because of this trouble, the "rowdy" element was there in force and he feared that they might make themselves unpleasant to Dickens.

But nothing untoward occurred at Washington. Indeed, the four Readings given there were among the most successful of the tour. Dickens told Forster: "The audiences here are really fine. So ready to laugh or cry and doing both so freely that you would suppose them to be Manchester shillings rather than Washington half-sovereigns." The first Reading, on 3 February, was a brilliant occasion, attended by the President, the Cabinet, the Supreme Court and all the Ambassadors. Because of a faulty gas supply, the platform was badly lighted, and in a short preliminary speech Dickens told his distinguished audience that he would trust to the brightness of their faces for the illumination of his own.

In Washington, on 7 February, he celebrated his fifty-sixth birthday. His letter to Georgina was dated, "My Birthday, 1868 (and my cold worse than ever)." It was now in his throat and on his chest. He spent the entire day in his rooms, except for a short excursion to the White House for an audience with the President. All America seemed to have remembered his birthday. Letters of congratulation, telegrams, cards, presents poured in from all over the country. His sitting-room was filled with flowers.

Charles Sumner, an old friend, called in the afternoon to congratulate him and found him covered with mustard poultices, apparently voiceless. Sumner turned to Dolby and said, "Surely, Mr. Dolby, you are not going to allow Mr. Dickens to read tonight." Dolby replied, "I have told Mr. Dickens at least a dozen times today that it will be impossible for him to read; and but for my knowledge of him and of his wonderful power of changing when he gets to the little table, I should be even more anxious about him than I am." Dickens found this return of energy whenever he came face to face with his audiences a source of great confidence, "but," he told Fields, "I am not at times without the nervous dread that I may some day sink altogether." When he read that night, only those who knew him best detected the lack of voice. At the end of the Reading the ladies threw their bouquets

Phiz. David is disturbed while entertaining Traddles and Mr. and Mrs. Micawber (*David Copperfield*)

Phiz. Mr. Squeers and his pupils at the Saracen's Head (*Nicholas Nickleby*)

on to the platform and the men threw their button-holes, until he seemed to be standing in a garden of flowers.

At Washington he turned north for his farewell Readings in Baltimore and Philadelphia. In both towns the people could not believe that he was reading there for the last time. They were convinced that the announcements of "farewell Readings" must be a publicity stunt and that there would be more Readings later on. From Philadelphia on 13 February he told Georgina: "Nothing will induce the people to believe in the farewells. At Baltimore on Tuesday night (a very brilliant night indeed) they asked as they came out: 'When will Mr. Dickens read here again?' 'Never.' 'Nonsense! Not come back, after such houses as these? Come. Say when he'll read again?' Just the same here. We could as soon persuade them that I am the President, as that tomorrow night I am going to read here for the last time."

The next stage of the tour lay to the north-east, where, during the third week in February, Dickens was scheduled to read in the New England towns of New Haven, Hartford and Providence. Dolby had intended to superintend the sale of tickets in these towns, but Dickens, not wishing to lose his company, had asked him to stay with him during the Baltimore and Philadelphia farewells. Dolby, therefore, had telegraphed his deputy, Kelly, in New York, telling him to handle the sale of the tickets. The day after Dickens and Dolby arrived in Baltimore, they were astounded to read in the newspapers that a riot had occurred at the sale of tickets in New Haven, that the mayor of New Haven had accused Dickens of swindling the public and that an "indignation meeting" was to be held in the town.

Dolby set off immediately for New Haven, calling first at New York to interview Kelly. It did not take him long to discover that Kelly had acted dishonestly at New Haven. He had sold the eight front rows to the speculators before selling to the public. When the people in the queue realised what was happening, they attacked the speculators and there was hand-to-hand fighting in the streets. Kelly had made his escape from the town, leaving

I

most of the speculators in the cells of the police station. After making sure that the sales of tickets at Hartford and Providence had been conducted honestly, Dolby left for New Haven.

He arrived in time for the indignation meeting and was greeted with much abuse. The Mayor of New Haven, who was in the chair, established his impartiality at the outset of the meeting by stating that until the present dispute he had never heard of Charles Dickens in his life and consequently had no personal feelings in the matter, but he hated any kind of swindle. Dolby took the wind out of the meeting by announcing that Dickens would not read in New Haven until there was another distribution of tickets approved by all the town. He also announced that the money taken that week would be returned the following day at the advertised prices. This did not suit the many people who had bought their tickets from the speculators at high prices, but Dolby could not be moved. After returning the money he received a delegation of prominent citizens led by the Mayor, who asked him to induce Dickens to give another date to the town. Dickens told Georgina: "Dolby and the Mayor of New Haven alternately embrace and exchange mortal defiances." Dolby was aware that the people of New Haven had a real grievance and he promised to do all he could. Then he travelled to New York and sacked Kelly. Dickens told Wills: "Here is another Paragon found out! The fellow (speculating himself) is at the bottom of all the troubles we have had, and has not only made me appear in this town the most grasping and sordid scoundrel going, but has cost me in this one place £300." Eventually Dickens agreed to give another date to New Haven.

The remaining Readings for that week in New England, at Hartford and Providence, went well, but travelling conditions were miserable. The winter was proving to be one of the severest on record. The weather was bitterly cold and the country was covered in deep snow. At the end of the week Dickens was glad to return to the comforts of the Parker House in Boston. Osgood, who had been superintending the sale of tickets in upstate New

York, where Dickens was scheduled to read in the middle of March, had also returned to Boston and he reported that at Rochester and Buffalo, both towns near the frontier, Canadians had struggled over the frozen river and clambered over all sorts of obstacles to buy tickets.

Dickens had intended to give eight Readings in Boston during the last week in February and the first week in March, four of which had been announced; but because of the unsettled political situation, the sale of tickets for the advertised Readings had not been up to the standard of the previous Readings in Boston. He decided, therefore, not to give the last four Readings, but to take a week's holiday instead. He hoped that by the time he resumed reading the political excitement would have abated.

Since Dickens left Washington, the political storm had burst and the impeachment of President Johnson was all but certain. People talked of nothing else. Political discussion was one of the most popular recreations in America and in an exciting situation such as this even Dickens had to take a back seat. The impeachment vote was held at five o'clock on Monday, 24 February, the night of the first Boston Reading. That night the three largest theatres in the town played to almost empty houses and the usual long line of people outside the Tremont Temple, hoping for a returned ticket for the Reading, was nowhere to be seen.

By the third Reading, however, business had picked up again. Dickens told Georgina: "The Boston audiences have come to regard the Readings and the reader as their peculiar property; and you would be at once amused and pleased if you could see the curious way in which they seem to plume themselves on both. They have taken to applauding too whenever they laugh or cry, and the result is very inspiriting." He read them the *Carol*. "They took it so tremendously that I was stopped every five minutes. One poor girl in mourning burst into a passion of grief about Tiny Tim, and was taken out."

It was during this stay in Boston that the "Great International

Walking Match" was held. Dolby and Osgood, who were always thinking up ways of diverting Dickens, had decided at the beginning of February to have a walking match. This had begun as a joke, but Dickens characteristically threw himself completely into the affair. He drew up the burlesque "Articles of Agreement" between "George Dolby, British subject, *alias* the Man of Ross and James Ripley Osgood, American citizen, *alias* the Boston Bantam". The umpires and starters and declarers of victory were to be "James T. Fields, of Boston, known in sporting circles as Massachusetts Jemmy and Charles Dickens, of Falstaff's Gad's Hill, whose surprising performances (without the least variation) on that truly national instrument, the American catarrh, have won for him the well-merited title of the Gad's Hill Gasper." The course was to lie six and a half miles along the Mill Dam Road to Newton Centre and back. It was also agreed that the Gasper should write a "sporting narrative" of the match within one week of its coming off and that he should give a dinner to all concerned.

The race took place on 29 February and Dickens accompanied the contestants over the course. In the "sporting narrative" he described the race, which began "in the teeth of an intensely cold and bitter wind, before which the snow flew fast and furious across the road from right to left". The "knowing eye" of the sporting chronicler had not failed to detect "considerable disparity between the lads". The Boston Bantam (*alias* Bright Chanticleer) was "a young bird, though too old to be caught with chaff". He came of "a thorough game breed" and had "a clear though modest crow". He pulled down the scales at "ten stone and a half and add a pound or two". The Man of Ross was "a thought and a half too fleshy" and had he "accidentally sat down upon his baby" he would have done so "to the tune of fourteen stone".

At first the Boston Bantam had a slight lead, but the Man of Ross "responded to the challenge and soon breasted him". For the first three miles the walking was very even. At four miles the men were side by side, ploughing up a hill through heavy snow. "At this point it was anybody's game, a dollar on Rossius and two half-dollars on the member of the feathery tribe." At five miles the men were still shoulder to shoulder. At six miles Dickens put on a tremendous spurt to leave them behind and establish himself at the turning point. On taking his station and turning about, he received "a mental knock-downer" to find "Bright Chanticleer close in upon him, and Rossius steaming up like a locomotive". The Boston Bantam rounded first and from that moment shot steadily ahead and "pegged away with his little drumsticks as if he saw his wives and a peck of barley waiting for him at the family perch". The Great International Walking Match was over and America had won. The day was so cold that by the end of the race "heads of hair, beards, eyelashes and eyebrows were frozen into icicles".

At the end of his second week in Boston Dickens, accompanied by Dolby, set off on a tour of mainly one-night stands in the smaller towns of New York State and New England. This tour was to occupy the remaining three weeks in March and was to involve him in some hard travelling. All trains from Boston were running late because of the heavy snow and to avoid delay they started a day earlier. They drove from the hotel to the railway station in a sleigh. Dickens told Macready that he had been sleighing so much that he was "sick of the sound of a sleigh bell". It was a miserable journey to Syracuse with a gale of wind blowing and snow falling heavily. After the exertions of the Great International Walking Match, his catarrh had taken "a fresh start, as if it were quite a novelty" and was worse than ever.

On this railway journey, as on all the others he made during the American tour, he was struck by the reserve of his fellow-passengers towards him compared to the impudent intrusions on his privacy he had to endure twenty-five years previously. He told Forster: "In the railway cars, if I see anybody who clearly wants to speak to me, I usually anticipate the wish by speaking myself. If I am standing on the brake outside (to avoid the intolerable stove), people getting down will say with a smile: 'As I am taking my departure, Mr. Dickens, and can't trouble you for more than a moment, I should like to take you by the hand, sir,' and so we shake hands and go our ways."

At Syracuse he stayed in a most uncomfortable hotel. He told Fields: "The awakening to consciousness this morning on a lopsided bedstead facing nowhere, in a room holding nothing but sour dust, was the more terrible than the being afraid to go to bed last night. To keep ourselves up we played whist (double rummy) until neither of us could bear to speak to the other any more. We had previously supped on a tough old nightmare named buffalo." Among other delicacies on the menu were "Fowl de poulet", "Paettie de Shay", "Celary" and "Murange with cream". When Dickens asked the Irish waiter what "Paettie de Shay" was, he was told it was the "Frinch name the steward giv' to oyster pattie". It could be washed down with any one of a number of items on the wine list, including "Mouseaux", "Table Madeira", "Abasinthe" and "Curaco". Dickens told Fields: "I mean to drink my love to Mrs. Fields after dinner in Mouseaux. Your ruggeder nature shall be pledged in Abasinthe."

At Rochester they found the town threatened by floods. A sudden thaw had caused blocks of ice to flow down the river and form an enormous ridge above the Genesee Falls. The people had been up all night, ready to move at a moment's notice. Boats were drawn up in the streets, with piles of household goods beside them. In the basement of the hall, where Dickens was to read, there was already three feet of water. The fear of floods affected the attendance and the receipts of $1,906 were among the lowest of the tour. In the dead of night the ice ridge collapsed with a thundering noise. The swollen river rolled down the Falls and the danger was over.

From Rochester they travelled to Buffalo. Dickens, who always had an eye for a pretty face, reported to Forster that in Buffalo, as in other towns near the frontier, "the American female beauty dies out; and a woman's face clumsily compounded of German,

Irish, Western American, and Canadian, not yet fused together, and not yet moulded, obtains instead. Our show of Beauty at night is generally remarkable; but we had not a dozen pretty women in the whole throng last night, and the faces were all blunt."

The two Buffalo Readings were followed by a short pleasure trip to Niagara Falls. The best view of the Falls was to be seen from the Canadian side, but because of the severity of the winter the hotel on that side was closed and Dickens had to be content with the American view. On his last day at Niagara he clambered up to a position above the river, where he could see the waters as they rushed forward to the Falls. He described the scene to Forster: "All away to the horizon on our right was a wonderful confusion of bright green and white water. As we stood watching it with our faces to the top of the Falls, our backs were towards the sun. The majestic valley below the Falls, so seen through the vast cloud of spray, was made of rainbow. The high banks, the riven rocks, the forests, the bridge, the buildings, the air, the sky, were all made of rainbow. Nothing in Turner's finest water-colour drawings, done in his greatest day, is so ethereal, so imaginative, so gorgeous in colour, as what I then beheld – I seemed to be lifted from the earth and to be looking into Heaven."

From Niagara he travelled to Rochester to give a second Reading there. Wherever he read, the local newspapers printed columns of description about him. He told Fechter: "Every night I read I am described (mostly by people who have not the faintest notion of observing) from the sole of my boot to where the top-most hair of my head ought to be but is not. Sometimes I am described as being 'evidently nervous'; sometimes it is rather taken ill that 'Mr. Dickens is so extraordinarily composed'. My eyes are blue, red, grey, white, green, brown, black, hazel, violet, and rainbow-coloured. I am like 'a well-to-do American gentle-man', and the Emperor of the French, with an occasional touch of the Emperor of China, and a deterioration of the attributes of our

famous townsman, Rufus W. B. D. Dodge Grumsher Pickville.
I say all sorts of things that I never said, go to all sorts of places
that I never saw or heard of, and have done all manner of things
(in some previous state of existence I suppose) that have quite
escaped my memory."

On 17 March they left Rochester for Albany, where Dickens
was scheduled to give two Readings. The conductor of the train
told them that he was doubtful about getting through, because
with the rapid thaw the country was flooded for three hundred
miles. They reached Utica in the early afternoon to find the
greater part of the town under water. It was impossible to
proceed any farther and they booked in at the local hotel. The
delay was not to affect the Albany Readings, because Dolby had
taken the precaution of allowing an extra day for travelling.
With the prospect of being called at any hour to continue the
journey, it seemed pointless to go to bed, so they passed the time
playing cribbage and double rummy. At six the following morning they were told to "get aboard and try it". Half an hour later
they were told that there was "no sort o' use" in getting aboard
and trying it. But at eight o'clock it was decided to make the
attempt and all the bells in the town were rung to summon the
passengers together.

The train crawled through the flood waters at four miles an
hour. On the way they rescued the passengers from two trains
which had been in the waters for the previous day and night.
Then they came across a train loaded with cattle and sheep. The
beasts had become so hungry that they had started to eat each
other. They towed the train to a dry spot and released the
animals. Dickens told Fields: "I never could have realised the
strong and dismal expressions of which the faces of sheep are
capable, had I not seen the haggard countenances of this unfortunate flock as they tumbled out of their dens and picked themselves up and made off, leaping wildly (many with broken legs)
over a great mound of thawing snow, and over the worried body
of a deceased companion. Their misery was so very human that I

was sorry to recognise several intimate acquaintances conducting themselves in this forlornly gymnastic manner."

The official in charge of the stretch of railway assured Dickens that if he could be "got along", he was the man to get him along. Then he turned out his full gang of a hundred men. They waded in front of the train, each armed with a long pole, and pushed the blocks of ice from the track. In this manner the train reached dry land at last and arrived in Albany at six o'clock in the evening. The journey which usually took three hours had taken ten. Neither Dickens, Dolby, nor their staff of five men had been in bed the previous night, nor had they had anything to eat since morning, but they set to work immediately and within two hours the hall was ready for the Reading. That night Dickens read the *Carol* and the *Pickwick Trial* with all his customary vigour.

But he was tiring rapidly. Since his visit to Niagara, the old trouble had broken out in his left foot and it was never to leave him for the remainder of his stay in America. It lamed him and made walking very painful. He longed for the tour to end, but he still had six one-night stands to make in Springfield, Worcester, New Haven, Hartford, New Bedford and Portland before beginning the farewell Readings in Boston and New York.

In New Haven the bad feeling over the previous sale of tickets had died away and a few well-chosen words by Dickens before the Reading put everyone in a good humour. The weather had turned cold again and there were frequent snow storms. With the return of the snow, his catarrh, which had been lulled by the milder weather, came back as bad as ever. He coughed from two or three in the morning until daybreak, when he usually fell into an exhausted sleep. On the morning he should have left for New Bedford he was so tired that he could not get up and he had to take the chance of an afternoon train getting him there on time. On the morning after the New Bedford Reading, he forced himself to get up early in order to make the long journey to Portland.

From Portland he told Forster: "I am nearly used up. Climate, distance, catarrh, travelling, and hard work, have begun (I may say so, now they are nearly over) to tell heavily upon me." But he had no thought of giving in and he found a like spirit in the people of Portland. "I write in a town three parts of which were burnt down in a tremendous fire three years ago. The people lived in tents while their city was rebuilding. The charred trunks of the trees with which the streets of the old city were planted, yet stand here and there in the new thoroughfares like black spectres. The rebuilding is still in progress everywhere. Yet such is the astonishing energy of the people that the large hall in which I am to read tonight (its predecessor was burnt) would compare very favourably with the Free Trade Hall at Manchester!" After his return from Portland to Boston the hard travelling was over. Only the Boston and New York farewell Readings remained before he sailed for home on 22 April.

Dickens was glad he had decided not to go on reading into May. He was convinced that had he done so he would have broken down. He told Forster: "It was well that I cut off the Far West and Canada when I did. There would else have been a bad complication. It is impossible to make the people about one understand, however zealous and devoted (it is impossible even to make Dolby understand until the pinch comes) that the power of coming up to the mark every night, with spirits and spirit, may co-exist with the nearest approach to sinking under it."

Between the 1st and the 8th of April he gave six farewell Readings in Boston. The nearest he came to collapsing was on the day of the third Reading. He had been unwell since morning and at four o'clock in the afternoon it was still doubtful whether he would be able to read. Longfellow and Fields urged him not to, but he was determined to read that night. By the time he reached the hall his foot was so painful that he needed the help of Dolby's arm to get to the reading desk and back.

He was hardly eating any solid food and to keep up his strength he established a routine. At seven in the morning, in bed, he had a tumbler of fresh cream and two tablespoonfuls of rum. At noon he had a sherry cobbler and a biscuit. At three o'clock he had a pint of champagne, and at five minutes to eight, before going on to the platform, an egg beaten up in a glass of sherry. In the intervals between the Readings he had a cup of strong beef tea and at quarter past ten a bowl of soup.

Dolby was anxious about his Chief. He never left the hall during the Readings, but sat by the side of the platform and kept his eyes upon Dickens all the time. Dickens told Mamie: "Dolby is as tender as a woman and as watchful as a doctor." After the fourth Reading Dickens was more hopeful of being able to finish the tour. That night he had read *Copperfield* and *Bob Sawyer's Party*, the longest programme in the repertoire by quarter of an hour. Moreover, *Copperfield* was the most exhausting of all the Readings. Yet afterwards he felt far fresher than he had been for the past three weeks. He believed he had taken a turn for the better and his one fear was whether the catarrh had permanently damaged his lungs.

The final farewell Reading in Boston took place on Wednesday, 8 April, 1868. The Readings were *Doctor Marigold* and *Mrs. Gamp*. The receipts were $3,456, the largest for any Reading in America. This Reading yielded enormous profits not only for Dickens but also for "the noble army of speculators". Some ladies had gained access to the hall during the day and decorated the desk with flowers. Dickens thanked them saying: "Ladies and gentlemen, before allowing Doctor Marigold to tell his story in his own peculiar way, I kiss the kind fair hands unknown which have so beautifully decorated my table this evening." After the Reading, when the tumultuous applause had died away, Dickens said farewell to Boston. He told his audience that in this brief life it was "sad to do almost anything for the last time".

Five farewell Readings in New York remained before he sailed for home. He had also promised to attend a press dinner to be given in his honour at Delmonico's on 18 April. On the day of the dinner he had to call in Dr. Fordyce Barker. His foot had swollen to such an extent that he could not get his boot on.

Barker bandaged the foot carefully, but a difficulty was encountered in obtaining a gout stocking to go over the bandages. Dolby visited all the leading drug-stores without success. Wherever he went he was told that gout was unknown in New York. Late in the afternoon he heard of an Englishman, resident in the city, who suffered from gout. He sought him out and borrowed a gout stocking from him.

Dickens was more than an hour late when he entered the banquet room at Delmonico's on the arm of Horace Greeley. There were two hundred guests, the largest gathering of press men ever assembled in America. In his speech Dickens said that during this second visit to America he had been astounded at the amazing changes he had seen – "changes moral, changes physical, changes in the amount of land subdued and peopled, changes in the rise of vast new cities, changes in the growth of older cities almost out of recognition, changes in the graces and amenities of life, changes in the press, without whose advancement no advancement can be made anywhere". Nor was he so arrogant as to suppose that in the twenty-five years since his last visit there had been no changes in him and that he had "nothing to learn and no extreme impressions to correct". He wished to record that wherever he had been in America, "in the smallest places equally with the largest", he had been received with "unsurpassable politeness, delicacy, sweet temper, hospitality, consideration" and "unsurpassable respect" for his privacy. So long as he lived and so long as his descendants had any legal right in his books, this testimony would be republished as an appendix to every copy of *American Notes* and *Martin Chuzzlewit*, not "in mere love and thankfulness", but because he regarded it as "an act of plain justice and honour".

The last few days in America were spent getting the accounts in order. In all, a total of seventy-four Readings were given. Dolby's commission came to £2,888. Ticknor and Fields had a commission of £1,000, plus five per cent on all Boston receipts. The total expenses in America were $38,948, approximately

£13,000. The preliminary expenses were £614. Dickens's profit exceeded his most optimistic calculations, coming to the magnificent sum of £20,000.

On Monday, 20 April, 1868, the final farewell Reading of the tour took place in New York, when the *Carol* and the *Pickwick Trial* were given for the last time in America. The receipts were $3,298, the second largest of the tour. Dickens's farewell speech was listened to in rapt silence. He said that when he was reading *Copperfield* a few evenings previously, he had felt there was more than usual significance in the words of Peggotty, "My future life lies over the sea". He assured the audience that they would not pass from his mind, that he would often realise them as he saw them now, equally by his "winter fireside and in the green summer weather", and that he would never recall them as a mere public audience, but rather as a host of personal friends. "Ladies and gentlemen," he concluded, "I beg to bid you farewell. God bless you, and God bless the land in which I leave you." Then he turned and left the platform. The American tour was over.

On 22 April he sailed joyfully for home, but the future life which lay for him over the sea was to be short and sorrowful.

PART FOUR

The Farewell Tour 1868–70

Horrible thoughts of death – and shrouds with blood upon them – and a fear that has made me burn as if I was on fire – have been upon me all day. I was reading a book tonight, to while the time away, and the same things came into the print.

Sikes and Nancy

8

MURDEROUS INSTINCTS

DICKENS HAD decided even before he left for America that when he returned he would give a series of Farewell Readings in Britain and then "read No More". The terms offered by Chappells were even more liberal than those for the two previous British tours. At first they had proposed that Dickens should give seventy-five farewell Readings in London and the provinces for £6,000 plus "all expenses whatever", but this did not satisfy him entirely. He believed that the country could stand one hundred Readings. This was to be the last time he would read and at least that number would be needed to meet the demands of all the people who would want to hear him. He suggested this from Halifax *en route* to the United States. Chappells' approval reached him in Boston before the end of the first series of Readings there. Dickens agreed by return of post.

The temptation of a Farewell Tour was a great one. In less than a year he would be able to add £8,000 to the £20,000 earned in America. He was not a mercenary man, but he was very conscious of the needs of his family, and he still had three sons to provide for. The Farewell Tour would give him the opportunity to earn a great deal of money in a short time, far more than he could earn by writing. By reading he was rapidly making himself financially independent. These reasons, together with the satisfaction he found in reading publicly, made him discount the strain that such a hard tour would have on a constitution already weakened by his American experiences. As always he was reluctant to associate his state of health with the Readings.

The sea air on the voyage home had revived him so much that in a letter to his Boston friends he was able to describe himself as "brown beyond belief" and causing the greatest disappointment in all quarters by looking so well. "My doctor was quite broken down in spirits on seeing me for the first time last Saturday. *Good lord! seven years younger!* said the doctor recoiling."

But Forster, who saw him frequently that summer, noticed an abatement of his tremendous energy. The springing step had slowed and the wonderful brightness of his eyes was dimmed. One day, as he walked from his office to dine at Forster's house, he could read only the halves of the names over the shop doors that were on his right as he looked. He would attribute this to no other cause than the medicine he was taking. His right foot had become affected as well as his left, but Forster tells us that "all this disappeared upon any special cause for exertion; and he was never unprepared to lavish freely for others the reserved strength that should have been kept for himself. This indeed was the great danger for it dulled the apprehension of us all to the fact that absolute and pressing danger did positively exist."

Dickens allowed himself the briefest of rests after his return from America before flinging himself into a frenzy of business and social activities. W. H. Wills, his associate on *All the Year Round*, was absent through an accident on the hunting field. In addition to the editorial work, Dickens took over the financial side of the periodical. This had been in the sole charge of Wills. The work was new to Dickens and he had to master all the routines. In this crisis he was not content to let matters tick over until Wills's return. He made radical changes in the organisation of the periodical and began writing more frequently for it himself. He was also working on the legacy of his friend, Chauncey Hare Townshend, who had died recently, bequeathing him his papers with the request that he should edit them for publication. *No Thoroughfare*, which was still playing at the Adelphi, was produced in Paris early in June and Dickens travelled there to supervise the final rehearsals.

During that beautiful summer not a weekend passed when he did not entertain his friends at Gad's Hill. In this way he repaid some of the hospitality he had received in America. All his guests were met at the station by postillions dressed in the red jackets of the old Royal Dover Road. During their stay they were entertained by an elaborate series of picnics and outings arranged by Dickens for the greater pleasure of his guests.

He took a great interest in all the preparations for the Farewell Readings, which were scheduled to commence at the St. James's Hall on Tuesday, 6 October, 1868. To Chappells' advertisements he added this paragraph:

> It is scarcely necessary to add that any announcement made in connection with these Farewell Readings will be strictly adhered to and considered final; and that on no

Phiz. Nicholas thrashes Mr. Squeers (*Nicholas Nickleby*)

Phiz. Steerforth and David arrive unexpectedly at **Mr.** Peggotty's at
the time of Emily's betrothal to Ham (*David Copperfield*)

consideration whatever will Mr. Dickens be induced to appoint an extra night in any place in which he shall have been announced to read for the last time.

The emphatic wording of this paragraph left the public in no doubt of the finality of the tour and caused a rush on tickets to begin even before the titles of the Readings had been announced.

The autumn was made sad for Dickens by the departure of his son, Edward Bulwer Lytton Dickens (nicknamed Plorn) for Australia to join his brother, Alfred Tennyson Dickens, already settled there as a sheep farmer. Plorn was his favourite son and Dickens found it difficult to get over the separation. The commencement of the Farewell Readings came as a distraction to his troubled mind. Then a fortnight later he heard of the death of his last surviving brother, Frederick. Fred had always been a nuisance to him and a drain on his pocket, but this did not lessen his grief at the loss of his only brother. With the death of Fred coming so soon after the separation from Plorn, he had difficulty in rousing himself from his moods of deep depression.

The Farewell Tour began triumphantly, but from the start Dickens was exhausted. He was so easily nauseated after the nightly Readings that sometimes in the morning he could not even bear the taste in his mouth of the Tincture of Myrrh he used in cleaning his teeth. From Liverpool he told Forster: "I have not been well, and have been heavily tired. However, I have little to complain of – nothing, nothing; though, like Mariana, I am aweary." Dickens and Dolby now found themselves living the same kind of travelling life as before, but for Dolby the pleasure of it all was spoiled by his constant anxiety over Dickens. He feared that his Chief's health would break down as it had done in America.

Dickens's dread of railway travelling had been allayed to some extent by the slow American trains, but the resumption of journeys by British expresses brought back to him all the horrible memories of the Staplehurst accident. This accident had seriously affected his nervous system. He had sudden vague rushes of terror even when riding in a hansom cab. Before the accident he had thought nothing of driving a pair of horses through the busiest parts of London. Now he could not drive with any pleasure on the country lanes about Gad's Hill. During the railway journeys Dolby was always on the alert and when Dickens had one of these attacks, he would instantly produce a flask of brandy.

A General Election occurred in November and Chappells decided to suspend the Readings in the provinces during that month and confine them entirely to London. They feared that with the country obsessed by the election the business of the Readings would suffer. There was no indication of this happening when Dickens read at Liverpool and Manchester at the end of October. The receipts in both cities were enormous. Dickens welcomed the November break, not for the rest it would bring him, but because he would have time to perfect a Reading he had made from the murder in *Oliver Twist*.

Dickens had scarcely begun the Farewell Readings than he was seized by the conviction that a powerful novelty was needed to keep up the receipts in towns where he had read so often in the past. As this was the last tour he was to make, he was also anxious to give his audiences something to remember him by. The difficulty was to find a subject that would create such a sensation.

Five years previously he had fashioned a Reading from the final chapters of *Oliver Twist*, the ones that tell of the murder of Nancy by Bill Sikes. He adapted and cut the text with great care, but the result was so horrifying that he had been afraid to try it in public. He now decided to revive the idea of the 'Murder', as he called it, but he still doubted if it were suitable for reading publicly. He told Forster: "I have made a short reading of the murder in Oliver Twist. I cannot make up my mind, however, whether to do it or not. I have no doubt that I could petrify an audience by carrying out the notion I have of the way of rendering it. But whether the impression would not be so horrible as to keep them away another time, is what I cannot satisfy myself upon. What do you think?"

Forster did not like the idea. It seemed to him that such a subject was altogether outside the province of public reading. Dickens read the 'Murder' to Dolby. Unlike Forster, Dolby did not doubt its suitability; he knew it would be a great attraction, but he feared the effect of such a violent Reading on Dickens's health. He suggested that Dickens refer the matter to Chappells as they had the largest vested interest in the tour. Chappells were impressed by the 'Murder', but were inclined to give weight to Dickens's own fear that the Reading was so terrifying that people would not come a second time. To resolve this fear, it was decided that the 'Murder' should be given before a select audience whose opinion could be relied on. The date fixed for this private Reading was Tuesday, 17 November.

The decision to confine the Readings entirely to London during November gave Dickens time to rehearse the 'Murder'. As with all his Readings, he rehearsed it over and over again, sometimes three or four times a day, striving for the effects that would arouse passion and horror in his audience. One afternoon his son, Charley, was working in the library at Gad's Hill with the windows open. He was startled to hear in the garden a voice raised violently followed by screams. He rushed outside and saw his father murdering an imaginary Nancy with ferocious blows. At dinner he mentioned to his father what he had seen and Dickens acted it for him again. At the end he asked his son what he thought of it. "The finest thing I have ever heard," said Charley, "but don't do it." This puzzled Dickens, but Charley would give no reason for his verdict. He knew, too well, that his father would permit no reference to his failing health.

On Tuesday, 17 November, one hundred people gathered in the St. James's Hall. Each of them had received an invitation to "A Private Trial of the Murder in Oliver Twist". Among them were literary and theatrical people whose judgment Dickens considered worth having. Chappells had also invited reporters from the leading London newspapers. The audience clustered together in the front seats. They were a mere handful in the great auditorium.

The gas lamps were turned on, flooding the platform with bright light. Dickens came forward, took his place at the reading desk and opened his book. He had altered the usual arrangements on the platform. In addition to his back screen there were two large screens of the same maroon colour, set off, one at either side, like the wings at a theatre. This isolated his figure completely and made his slightest action clearly visible to the audience.

The Reading was in three short parts: 1. Where Fagin sets Noah Claypole to spy on Nancy. 2. The scene on London Bridge where Nancy talks to Mr. Brownlow and Rose Maylie. 3. Where Fagin rouses Claypole from his sleep to tell his twisted story to Sikes. And the murder of Nancy. From the beginning Dickens read with an intensity which gave reality to every scene. Four widely contrasted characters – Nancy, Bill Sikes, Noah Claypole and Fagin – were presented with such rapidity of sequence and alternation that they seemed to be before the audience not only in the flesh but also simultaneously.

They saw Nancy on London Bridge haunted by forebodings of death. They saw Noah Claypole, the tool of Fagin, long-limbed, bony and stupid. There was Fagin himself, high-shouldered with contracted chest, old, shrivelled and repulsive. And Bill Sikes, broad-built, surly and brutal. They watched Fagin, features distorted with rage, eyebrows working like the antennae of some deadly reptile, lips quivering passionately as he poured his venom into Sikes's ear. They heard him elicit the perverted story from Noah Claypole half-awake. They saw the dawning comprehension on Sikes's heavy face as the Jew hounded him on to the murder of Nancy. They heard the stentorian roars of Sikes when he believed that Nancy had betrayed him. They heard the evil triumph in Fagin's voice when, as Sikes rushed from the house, he stayed him for a moment with the words, "You won't be – you won't be – too – violent, Bill?" They heard the last gasping pleas of Nancy to "Bill, dear Bill", as she sank to her knees blinded by blood. They watched Sikes bring down the heavy club with all his force upon her upturned face. They watched, in terror, as he struck and struck again.

At the conclusion of the Reading the audience sat pale-faced and silent, but before they had a chance to collect their thoughts, the screens were whisked away to disclose a long table, with waiters ready to open oysters and bottles of champagne. Dickens invited the audience to come up on to the platform. The dresses of the ladies looked exquisite under the powerful lights. The whole scene was like a great bed of flowers and diamonds. It needed a diversion such as this to get the audience talking after the horrific experience they had undergone, but many of them were reluctant to express an opinion about the 'Murder'.

A women's doctor took Dickens aside and said: "My dear Dickens, you may rely upon it that if only one woman cries out when you murder the girl, there will be a contagion of hysteria all over this place." A celebrated critic said much the same thing. After describing the 'Murder' as "a most amazing and terrific thing", he added, "but I am bound to tell you that I had an almost irresistible impulse to scream, and that, if anyone had cried out, I am certain I should have followed".

Dickens turned to his son and asked: "Well, Charley, and what do you think of it now?" Charley replied: "It is finer even than I expected, but I still say, don't do it." At that moment Edmund Yates joined them. "What do you think of this, Edmund?" Dickens asked. "Here is Charley saying it is the finest thing he has ever heard, but persists in telling me, without any reason, not to do it." Yates gave Charley a quick look and, to Dickens's amazement, said gravely: "I agree with Charley, sir."

Dickens asked Mrs. Keeley, the actress: "What do *you* say? Do it or not?" She replied: "Why, of course, do it. Having got such an effect as that, it must be done." Then rolling her dark eyes slowly and speaking very distinctly, she added: "The public have been looking out for a sensation these last fifty years or so, and by Heaven they have got it!"

The private Reading had not resolved the question of whether the 'Murder' was suitable for reading publicly, and the only other way of finding the answer was to give the public the opportunity of hearing it. So Dickens and Chappells agreed that a public Reading should be given in London early in the New Year followed closely by a second Reading in Dublin, and that these two Readings would decide the fate of the 'Murder' once and for all.

In December, the General Election over, Dickens resumed his provincial tour. He intended to run off the remaining Readings without any rest whatever apart from a short break at Christmas. The London newspapers had carried long accounts of the 'Murder' Reading and its shadow fell over all the towns where he was announced to read. In Edinburgh many people asked that the 'Murder' be included in the Readings to be given there. But even though this request could not be granted, it made no difference to the Scottish receipts. In both Edinburgh and Glasgow every seat was taken and hundreds were turned away. From Edinburgh Dickens told Forster: "The affectionate regard of the people exceeds all bounds and is shown in every way. The audiences do everything but embrace me, and take as much pains with the Readings as I do. . . The keeper of the Edinburgh hall, a fine old soldier, presented me on Friday night with the most superb red camellia for my button-hole that ever was seen. Nobody can imagine how he came by it, as the florists had had a considerable demand for that colour, from ladies in the stalls, and could get no such thing."

Dickens enjoyed the Readings in Edinburgh and Glasgow, but his nerves had been badly shaken by the long railway journey to Edinburgh on the Flying Scotsman. He calculated that the trip had given thirty thousand shocks to his nervous system and the same agonies had to be endured again when he journeyed from

Scotland to London on Saturday, 19 December. The last Reading before his Christmas holiday took place at the St. James's Hall on Tuesday, 22 December. Before the Reading Dickens was tired and depressed. He doubted if he could manage to get through it. But when he stepped on to the platform, the energy, as always, came to him and that night he read especially well. Christmas week was not considered a profitable time for places of public entertainment, but even less astute promoters than Chappells would have risked a Reading of the *Carol* with the author standing at a reading desk decorated with sprigs of holly. When Dickens closed the book, two thousand people stood to applaud him.

By the beginning of January 1869 he had given twenty-eight of the hundred Readings. He told Collins: "I am perpetually counting the weeks before me to be 'read' through, and am perpetually longing for the end of them; and yet I sometimes wonder whether I shall miss something when they are over." Under the most favourable circumstances it would take him until the end of May to work off the remaining seventy-two Readings.

Dolby was worried by this pressure of time and by the possibility of interruptions through ill-health. He was convinced that only by the strictest observance of a routine and by taking precautions against accidents of any kind would Dickens be able to complete the tour. He was confident that he could arrange the travelling life to make his Chief as comfortable as possible. His greatest problem was Dickens's health, which had been so uncertain since the return from America. The pain in Dickens's foot kept recurring and was wearing him down. Because of this, Dolby was opposed to the 'Murder' Reading. He awaited the outcome of the first public Reading with alarm. He hoped the 'Murder' would be coldly received, for then Dickens's respect for the popular judgment would persuade him to abandon it. Dolby knew that nothing but that would carry any weight with him.

Since the private Reading of the 'Murder', Dickens had worked continuously on it, striving to make it as perfect as possible. He lengthened the Reading from thirty to forty minutes, the additional ten minutes being needed for the revised ending. The Reading had ended at a point almost immediately after the murder had been committed. Sikes had not moved from the room; he had been afraid to stir. He threw a rug over the body, but it was worse to fancy the eyes, and imagine them moving towards him, than to see them glaring upwards, so he plucked it off again. "And there was the body – mere flesh and blood, no more – but such flesh, and so much blood!" He thrust the club into the fire and was startled by a hair on the end of it, which blazed and shrunk into a light cinder and whirled up the chimney. He washed himself and rubbed his clothes, but he could not remove all the blood. There was blood all over the room. "The very feet of his dog were bloody." Dragging the dog with him, he shut the door and left the house. There the Reading had ended.

After the private Reading, Charles Kent had urged Dickens to add a description of the flight, so that the terror of Sikes might be more fully realised. At first Dickens was not convinced. "My dear fellow," he said, "believe me, no audience on earth could be held for ten minutes after the girl's death. Give them time, and they would be revengeful for having had such a strain put upon them. Trust me to be right. I stand there, and I know."

But, on reflection, Dickens agreed that such an ending would be an improvement. It would give a moral to the story which would redeem to some extent the sensational nature of the Reading. The problem was how to succeed in giving a description of the murderer's flight and destruction without detracting from the climax of the murder. He tried daily to devise an ending "with the object of rising from that blank state of horror into a fierce and passionate rush for the end". On 8 December he told Collins: "As yet I cannot make a certain effect of it; but when I shall have gone over it as many score of times as over the rest of that reading, perhaps I may strike one out."

By the end of the year he had succeeded with a masterly three-page condensation of the sections of the book which tell of the flight and death of Sikes. Nothing that could most powerfully convey the murderer's terror was missed out. "As he gradually left the town behind him all that day, and plunged that night into the solitude and darkness of the country, he was haunted by that ghastly figure following at his heels. He could hear its garments rustle in the leaves; and every breath of wind came laden with that last low cry. If *he* stopped, *it* stopped. If *he* ran, *it* followed; not running too – that would have been a relief – but borne on one slow melancholy air that never rose or fell.

"At times, he turned to beat this phantom off, though it should strike him dead; but the hair rose on his head, and his blood stood still, for it had turned with him, and was behind him then. He leaned his back against a bank, and felt that it stood above him, visibly out against the cold night sky. He threw himself on his back upon the road. At his head it stood, silent, erect and still: a human gravestone with its epitaph in Blood." When Dickens described the destruction of Sikes from the rooftop of the hideout in Jacob's Island, his voice was an avenging voice, not only against Sikes, but against all who had ever outraged the sanctity of human life.

Dickens hoped that this new ending would sublimate an incident of ghastly horror into an eloquent homily and so justify the Reading artistically. This was important to him. After the private Reading he was hurt by Forster's continued opposition to the 'Murder'. Dickens told him: "We might have agreed to differ about it very well, because we only wanted to find out the truth if we could, and because it was quite understood that I wanted to leave behind me the recollection of something very passionate and dramatic, done with simple means, if the art would justify the theme." Forster replied that it was impossible for him to admit that the effect produced was legitimate, or that it was desirable for Dickens to be remembered by such a Reading. He did not think the new ending redeemed in any way the horror of what had gone before. And to this extent Forster was right, that when the 'Murder' was performed publicly people came in their thousands to hear it, but for the sensation only, not for the moral.

Dickens rehearsed the new ending so often and immersed himself in it so completely that he admitted to having a vague sensation of being "wanted" as he walked about the streets. He still had his doubts about the Reading, wondering if it would not prove to be "too weird and woeful" for the general public. But all doubts were resolved at the first public Reading of *Sikes and Nancy*, as it was now entitled, at the St. James's Hall on Tuesday, 5 January, 1869. Throughout the Reading the audience sat frozen in their seats. It was not until after Dickens had left the platform that they came to life. Their shouts of approval penetrated the quiet of the dressing room, where he lay utterly exhausted on a sofa.

The following morning Dickens was tired but happy. He told his friend, Mary Boyle: "The crime being completely off my mind, and the blood spilled, I am (like many of my fellow-criminals) in a highly edifying state today." Dolby called on him that morning to make arrangements for their journey to Ireland, where Readings were scheduled in Dublin and Belfast. He congratulated Dickens on the success of *Sikes and Nancy*, but made no further reference to it. He saw no reason to say anything more. There would be plenty of time on the Irish journey to discuss the future of the 'Murder' as a stock Reading. But Dickens wanted to discuss it there and then. He asked Dolby's opinion on how frequently the 'Murder' should be performed. Dolby prevaricated. He reminded Dickens that the titles of the Readings were already announced for some weeks in advance. It would be a breach of faith to alter them. Dickens agreed, but insisted on one exception. He was due to read in Cheltenham on 23 January. As his old friend, Macready, lived in retirement there and was too feeble to come to London, the 'Murder' should be given in Cheltenham for his special benefit.

Dickens was looking forward to the Irish trip. It would give him the chance to meet old friends, especially his protégé, Percy

Fitzgerald. He was scheduled to give three Readings in Dublin and two in Belfast. With only two places to visit, the fatigue would not be great. Dolby had arranged for them to travel in easy stages and they had a fortnight before them.

In Dublin a large body of police was needed to control the crowds in the neighbourhood of the Rotunda. On the final night two hundred extra seats were brought in and the confusion was beyond control. It was impossible for Dickens to begin at the advertised time. To quell the riot he appeared on the platform and stood quietly by the reading desk. His presence had the effect of bringing the crowd to order and putting them in a good humour. The second public Reading of the 'Murder' took place in Dublin. It seemed to Dickens that the audience showed little appreciation, but Percy Fitzgerald assured him that the Reading had been a great success. In Belfast all tickets had been sold in advance. The Mayor and Corporation wanted to give a great banquet in his honour, but he would not agree as his visit was purely one of business.

Dickens and Dolby left Belfast by the mid-day train on Saturday, 16 January, to catch the mailboat from Kingstown that evening. Dickens was in better health than he had been for months, but an accident occurred that undid all the benefit of the Irish trip. Forty miles from Belfast the train shuddered violently. Looking out of the window they saw an enormous piece of iron flying alongside, carrying telegraph poles with it. They heard a crashing sound on the roof. Recalling the Staplehurst accident, Dickens threw himself on the floor. Then the train came to a halt and Dolby alighted to see what had happened. The great iron tyre of the driving wheel had broken and travelled backwards with tremendous force. A large piece had landed on the roof. They had to wait for an hour in a lonely spot for the arrival of another train to take them on to Dublin.

Dickens was very shaken and an important fortnight lay ahead. Readings were announced for London, Birmingham, Cheltenham, Clifton, Torquay and Bath. Dolby feared that the shock

Dickens had received might bring back the ailment to his foot. If these Readings had to be postponed, the loss to everyone concerned would be enormous. Dickens assured him that everything was all right, but Dolby suspected that only his Chief's willpower could prevent a catastrophe. He reported to Chappells that all looked well for a prosperous fortnight, but his own mind was filled with doubts and misgivings.

During the first week of that fortnight Dickens read *Sikes and Nancy* at Cheltenham for the benefit of Macready. The old actor was very infirm. Throughout the Reading he sat on the front row staring grimly at Dickens. After it was over he could not find words to express his admiration. "It comes to this," he finally declared, "TWO MACBETHS!" Then he looked defiantly at Dolby as if Dolby had contradicted him. Macready's compliment flattered Dickens and he often repeated it to his friends.

The following week in the West Country was easier. The journeys were short and the towns, with the exception of Bath, were great favourites with Dickens. At the first Clifton Reading he gave what he described as "by far the best Murder yet done". He told Mamie: "At Clifton on Monday night we had a contagion of fainting; and yet the place was not hot. I should think we had from a dozen to twenty ladies taken out stiff and rigid at various times! It became quite ridiculous."

After Clifton there was nothing to do until the Wednesday when the Torquay Reading was to be given. They left Clifton early to give Dickens as much time as possible in Torquay. His room at the hotel was comfortable and overlooked the sea. The weather was warm and although only the end of January, the vegetation was as far advanced as it was in the Midlands and the North early in May. He was able to enjoy some long walks beside the sea. It was more of a pleasure than a business trip. The demand for tickets was enormous and the Readings, *Doctor Marigold* and the *Pickwick Trial*, caused him little exertion.

The Torquay Reading was one of the most brilliant of the Farewell Tour. The receipts were nearly £270, the highest total in the history of entertainment in the town. Bath was the only place that cast a shadow over the week. Dickens did not like reading in Bath. He had never done as well there as in other towns. They arrived in pouring rain. He told Forster: "The place looks to me like a cemetery which the dead have succeeded in rising and taking. Having built streets of their old gravestones, they wander about scantily trying to 'look alive'." The local agent reported that bookings were not up to their usual standards, but could be considered good for Bath. However, the two Bath Readings went better than anticipated and it was in Bath that he learned that his son, Sydney, an officer in the Navy, had been appointed a first lieutenant aboard a new ship. This news sent him back to London in good spirits and so ended one of the happiest weeks in his reading career. But a fortnight after his return from the West Country the first breakdown of the tour occurred.

On Monday, 15 February, Dickens had the worst attack in his left foot that he had ever had, even worse than those he had suffered in America. A Reading had been announced for the following evening at the St. James's Hall and the day after that he was scheduled to leave again for Scotland for the final Farewells in Edinburgh and Glasgow. On Tuesday his doctor, Frank Carr Beard, together with Sir Henry Thompson, the surgeon, were called in. They forbade him to read that night. They told him that it would be physically impossible for him to stand, let alone read, and they issued a medical certificate stating: "We the undersigned hereby certify that Mr. Charles Dickens is suffering from inflammation of the foot (caused by over-exertion), and that we have forbidden his appearance on the platform this evening, as he must keep his room for a day or two."

The cancellation of the London and Scottish Readings distressed Dickens. He knew that this would inconvenience hundreds of people and also mean a great loss for Chappells. He told Forster: "Heaven knows what engagements this may involve in

April! It throws us all back and will cost me some five hundred pounds." By the time the medical certificate was issued it was two o'clock in the afternoon and Dolby had still to announce the cancellation of the Reading scheduled for eight o'clock that evening. The majority of those who had bought tickets did not learn the news until they arrived at the St. James's Hall for the performance, yet many of them were more concerned about Dickens's health than their own disappointment. After returning the money, Dolby left immediately for Scotland to postpone the Readings announced for Glasgow and Edinburgh. Fortunately he had two clear days before him in Glasgow and three in Edinburgh. This was just as well, for there had been an unprecedented sale of tickets in both cities.

Meanwhile in London Dickens chafed at the restrictions placed upon him. To Dolby he wrote: "You know how earnestly I hope to get sword in hand again and that soon, and fight it out. I am as restless as if I were behind bars in the Zoological Gardens, and if I could afford it would wear a part of my mane away as the Lion has done by rubbing it against the windows of my cage."

After a few days' rest the swelling and the pain in his foot abated, and on Saturday, 20 February, he left London for Edinburgh. He told Forster: "I came down lazily on a sofa, hardly changing my position the whole way. The railway authorities had done all sorts of things and I was more comfortable than on the sofa at the hotel." When Dolby learned by telegram that Dickens was on his way, he announced to the press that the Readings would be given the following week. But when he met Dickens off the train, he was distressed to see that he was very lame and that his face still bore the traces of the severe pain he had undergone. Dickens was in high spirits and he assured Dolby that apart from the temporary inconvenience there was not much the matter.

But the next day the foot became troublesome again. Dickens was in such agony that he sent for Mr. Syme, the celebrated Edinburgh surgeon. Syme had been the tutor of Sir Henry

Thompson and he completely rejected his old pupil's diagnosis of gout. Dickens told Georgina: "Syme repeated 'Gout!' with the greatest indignation and contempt several times." Syme declared the condition to be an affection of the delicate nerves and muscles originating in cold. This diagnosis pleased Dickens, who had an aversion to the idea of having gout. He reported to Forster the conversation with Syme: "I told him that it had shown itself in America in the other foot as well. 'Now I'll just swear,' said he, 'that beyond the fatigue of the readings you'd been tramping in the snow within two or three days.' I certainly had. 'Well,' said he triumphantly, 'and how did it first begin? In the snow. Gout? Bah! – Thompson knew no other name for it, and just called it gout. Bah!'"

Syme recommended complete rest. He also prescribed a special kind of boot, which did succeed in giving Dickens some relief. But Thompson's diagnosis of gout was nearer the truth than that of his master, Syme, who believed the condition to be only a local one. Syme's diagnosis was to have unfortunate consequences, for it gave Dickens the justification for disregarding the grave warnings in his foot.

There was great excitement in Scotland over the Final Farewell Readings. Tickets could have been sold at twice the price. Everyone wanted to hear the 'Murder'. Since the first public Reading of *Sikes and Nancy*, Dickens had continued working at it. The 'Murder' had become an obsession with him. He told Dolby that "it must be set apart from all our other effects and judged by no other Reading standard". His friends feared that a too frequent repetition might permanently damage his health, but he ignored all advice. Dolby wrote: "The horrible perfection to which he brought it acted as a charm to him and made him the more determined to go on with it come what might."

In Edinburgh the interest in the 'Murder' was so great that all the seats were booked in advance and the shilling places were filled within minutes of the doors opening. The expectant silence in which the vast audience waited for the Reading to begin affected Dickens and he read more vehemently than on any previous occasion. He worked himself up to such a pitch that he drove all the breath out of his body. When he left the platform he fell into the arms of Dolby who, together with Scott, Dickens's valet, supported him to his dressing-room. They laid him on a sofa, where he gasped for breath, unable to utter a word. But he allowed himself no more than the customary ten-minute break. After a glass of iced brandy-and-soda (he had renounced champagne), he went on for the final Reading with a light step, as though he were just beginning the evening's work. He liked to follow *Sikes and Nancy* with a comic Reading such as *Mrs. Gamp* or the *Pickwick Trial* to offset all the horror and to send the audience out into the night in a light-hearted mood.

The friends who came round to the dressing-room after the Reading were so overcome by what he jokingly referred to as his "murderous instincts", that they did not know how to congratulate him. One of them who, unable to obtain a ticket, had been given a seat behind the screen, was nearly frightened off the platform by the 'Murder'. He sat in the dressing-room staring wild-eyed at Dickens over a glass of champagne. The uneasiness of these friends, coupled with their concern for his health, made them decline his invitation to have supper with him, and Dolby and he were left to dine alone.

That night, during supper, Dickens suggested to Dolby that they fix the Readings for the remainder of the tour. They went on with their meal, each making notes of the Readings Dickens was choosing for the various towns. When they had got through about sixteen of these, Dolby noticed that *Sikes and Nancy* was taking precedence over all other Readings and was down to be given three or even four times a week. He pointed this out to Dickens, arguing that as the success of the tour was assured it would not make a bit of difference to the profits which Readings were given. The public, in their desire to hear him read for the last time, would come in the same numbers for an old favourite as they would for the 'Murder'. The *Carol*, *Nickleby* or *Doctor*

Marigold would produce all the money they could take and Dickens would be saved the agony of tearing himself to pieces three or four nights a week. He suggested to Dickens that if he wished to do the 'Murder' he should reserve it for a few of the large cities.

Dickens jumped up from his chair in a paroxysm of rage. He threw his knife and fork down on his plate with such force that he shattered it, and shouted: "Dolby, your infernal caution will be your ruin one of these days." Dolby had never seen him in such a rage and he waited quietly for the storm to pass. Then Dickens began to sob bitterly. He came towards Dolby, embraced him affectionately and apologised.

Dickens was so ill in Edinburgh that Dolby feared that he would not get through the week. He did complete his Readings there, but the pain this cost him could be seen in his worn face. Before they left Edinburgh for Glasgow Syme was again consulted. He had no remedy to offer except complete rest. With all the work ahead, this was the one thing that was impossible. After a triumph in Glasgow as great as that in Edinburgh they returned to London on Saturday, 27 February. On the following Tuesday Dickens was to "commit the murder" for the second time at the St. James's Hall. The reputation of the Reading caused a great run on tickets and the Hall was crammed.

Edmund Yates described the Reading in *Tinsleys' Magazine*: "Gradually warming with excitement he flung aside his book and acted the scene of the murder, shrieked the terrified pleadings of the girl, growled the brutal savagery of the murderer, brought looks, tones, gestures simultaneously into play to illustrate his meaning, and there was not one of those who had known him best or who believed in him most, but was astonished at the power and versatility of his genius."

Writing of the Jew as represented on the stage by contemporary actors, Yates said: "Fagin, as shown by Mr. Dickens is very different from any of these. There is nothing comic about him, there is nothing grand or tragic as in Shylock; he is sordid,

L

mean, avaricious, and revengeful, and Mr. Dickens shows him to you in every phase. You read it in his rounded shoulders, in his sunken chin, in his pinched cheeks and hanging brow, in his gleaming eyes, and quivering clutching hands, in the lithe shiftiness of his movements, and the intense earnestness of his attitudes. The voice is husky and with a slight lisp, but there is no nasal intonation; a bent back, but no shoulder-shrug; the conventional attributes are omitted, the conventional words are never spoken; and the Jew fence, crafty and cunning even in his bitter vengeance, is here before us to the life."

Describing the Murder scene, Yates wrote: "It is here of course that the excitement of the audience is wrought to its highest pitch, and that the acme of the actor's art is reached. The raised hands, the bent-back head, are good; but shut your eyes and the illusion is more complete. Then the cries for mercy, the "Bill! dear Bill! for dear God's sake!" uttered in tones in which the agony of fear prevails even over the earnestness of the prayer, the dead, dull voice as hope departs, are intensely real. When the pleading ceases, you open your eyes in relief, in time to see the impersonation of the murderer seizing a heavy club and striking his victim to the ground."

On the Saturday of the same week the 'Murder' was committed for the first time in Manchester. The Free Trade Hall was larger than the St. James's Hall and this made any Reading there a great strain. Before the Reading Dickens tested the 'Murder' in the empty auditorium. He was relieved to find that without much greater expenditure of voice and by enlarging the action a little he could get all the effects he wanted. But there was one other possible hazard of reading the 'Murder' in so large a hall. For a full appreciation of the Reading, concentration and absolute silence were necessary. He was worried that some incident would occur such as a person screaming with fright, or the dropping of a stick or umbrella. Any interruption took the attention of the audience off him and in that immense place he would have to work hard to get it back.

Fortunately no such incident did occur and the Manchester Reading was as successful as the London one. Dickens reported to Georgina that "the go throughout was enormous". The manner in which different audiences reacted to the 'Murder' fascinated him. In the same letter he wrote: "As always happens now – and did not at first – they were unanimously taken by Noah Claypole's laugh." He told Fields: "In the country the people usually collapse with the murder, and don't fully revive in time for the final piece; in London, where they are much quicker, they are equal to both." The reaction of the Dublin audience had puzzled him. They received the 'Murder' so quietly that Percy Fitzgerald had to assure him that it had been a great success. He told Fitzgerald: "It is extraordinarily difficult to understand (from the point of action) an audience that does not express itself, and I certainly mistook mine on Wednesday night. When the 'Murder' was done in London, the people were frozen while it went on, but came to life when it was over and rose to boiling point." Dickens had persuaded himself that *Sikes and Nancy* was his most powerful and effective Reading. It was gruesome enough, but some critics thought it overstrained and much preferred the delicacy of the other Readings. His young friend, Percy Fitzgerald, thought it far too melodramatic.

Whenever the 'Murder' was performed it produced the same dangerous symptoms in Dickens. Dolby wrote: "That the frequency with which he persisted in giving this Reading was affecting him seriously, nobody could judge better than myself, living and travelling with him as I was, day after day and week after week." Dolby had noticed that the shocks the Reading gave to Dickens's nervous system were not easily overcome. They would recur later on after the performance, either in great hilarity or in a craving to be on the platform again. But nothing could shake Dickens's determination to continue with the 'Murder'. In March he told Mamie: "The foot goes famously. I feel the fatigue of it (four Murders in one week) but not over much. It merely aches at night; and so does the other, sympathetically, I suppose."

The next town after Manchester was Hull, where he was to read for two nights. From Hull he was to go on to York for one night. He would then return to London on Friday, 12 March. This would give him three clear days before his next engagement at the St. James's Hall on the following Tuesday. It seemed likely that at last he would get some of the rest he so desperately needed. But an unexpected exertion intervened. At Hull he learned of the death of Sir James Emerson Tennent, the old friend to whom he had dedicated his latest book, *Our Mutual Friend*. In his tired state the news unnerved him completely. He even wondered whether the Hull and York Readings would not have to be cancelled. But he was determined to do his duty by Chappells. He was equally determined to attend the funeral of his friend.

At first the difficulties of getting to London in time for the funeral seemed insurmountable. The night train left York at a quarter to ten and the Reading would not be over before ten o'clock. Time was needed to change his clothes and the hall was a ten minute drive from the railway station. By then the Great Northern express would be on its way.

He found a solution, but it was one that entailed self-sacrifice on his part. Dolby arranged with the station master at York to hold the train for five minutes. A printed notice was circulated among the audience informing them that Dickens had been suddenly called to London; but not wishing to disappoint the people of York, he had determined on giving the Readings announced, dispensing with the time he usually took to himself for rest between each Reading. He began reading at eight o'clock precisely, before a distinguished audience led by the Archbishop of York. The three Readings were *Boots at the Holly Tree Inn*, *Sikes and Nancy* and *Mrs. Gamp*. Without missing a sentence or a gesture he went on with his performance as though he had all the time in the world. By giving up his breaks for rest he gained twenty minutes.

He finished reading at twenty minutes to ten and reached the station with two minutes to spare. A private saloon carriage had been booked for him and he changed from his evening dress on the way to London. At the funeral he appeared to Forster to be "dazed and worn", and when Dolby saw him later in the day he knew that more than three days' rest would be needed to revive him after the exertions of the previous night.

"Like lights in a theatre, they are being snuffed out fast," Dickens wrote to Fields on the progress of the Readings. Whether he was aware of it or not, this quotation from Carlyle on the guillotined of the French Revolution was grimly apposite to his own position. The Farewell Tour was a triumphal progress. In Birmingham in one night two thousand five hundred people came to hear him read for the last time. The receipts of the four farewell Readings in Liverpool exceeded one thousand pounds. His feet were tender and painful. He told Georgina that they often felt "as though they were in hot water". But he assured her that he was wonderfully well and strong and in "no end of voice". As in America the sleepless nights had returned. He would lie awake until daybreak. Wherever possible, Dolby arranged in the hotels to sleep in a bedroom with an adjoining door so that he could look in through the night and see how his Chief was getting on. He always found him awake but cheerful.

Much as he yearned for the tour to end, Dickens dreaded the empty months when he would not be reading. Already he was planning to fill them with activity. Fields was coming to Britain that summer and Dickens told him that he was making great plans for his entertainment: "I rather think that when the Twelfth of June shall have shaken off these shackles, there *will* be borage on the lawn at Gad's. Your heart's desire in that matter, and in the minor particulars of Cobham Park, Rochester Castle, and Canterbury, shall be fulfilled, please God! The red jackets shall turn out again upon the turn-pike road, and picnics among the cherry-orchards and hop-gardens shall be heard of in Kent."

The Farewell Tour was to terminate abruptly long before the

twelfth of June. After reading at the St. James's Hall on Tuesday, 13 April, the next towns were Leeds, Blackburn, Bolton, Preston and Warrington. On the morning of the London Reading Dickens suffered a severe haemorrhage from the piles which had troubled him off and on for some years. He asked Beard for a prescription for some medicine before setting off for the industrial towns of the north.

Edmund Yates called on Dickens at the Queens Hotel in Leeds and found him looking aged and worn. He was lying on a sofa. He had taken off his boot and the foot was swathed in bandages. The lines in his cheeks and round his eyes had always been noticeable, but now they were deep furrows. There was a weariness in his gaze and an air of depression about him. Yates was shocked by his appearance. Dickens tried to rouse himself for Yates's benefit, but he was obviously worn out and in much pain. He excused himself and went early to bed.

After the Leeds Readings Dolby arranged to spend two nights at Chester. He believed that the clean air of the picturesque old town would be better for Dickens than the smoky atmosphere of Blackburn, where he was to read next. On Saturday evening, 17 April, in his hotel room in Chester, Dickens became extremely giddy. When he tried to walk forward he found he had a tendency to go backwards. His left leg felt insecure. His left hand and arm were also strange. He tried to put something on the table, but only succeeded in pushing the table forward. If he did not look at anything he tried to touch with his left hand, he did not know where it was. When he came to brush his hair, he was reluctant to raise his hands to his head.

The symptoms persisted throughout the following day. The weather that day being fine and warm Dolby suggested a drive in the country. They drove to Mold, a small Welsh market town about fourteen miles from Chester. The country lanes were ablaze with spring blossom. Dickens sat silent and depressed. After a while he asked Dolby what he should do in the light of his condition. He was concerned about Chappells, whose losses would be great if any of the Readings had to be cancelled. Dolby assured him that Chappells would do everything in their power to adapt their arrangements to his state of health. Dickens decided that on his return to Chester he would write to Beard describing his symptoms and that while waiting for a reply he would watch the effect on himself of the next two Readings. Having reached these decisions, Dickens laid his head back on the seat and fell sound asleep. Dolby looked sadly at the sleeping face of his Chief. He knew instinctively that the travelling life was at an end.

The following day, Monday, 19 April, Dickens wrote to Beard giving an exact account of his symptoms. He asked if they could have been caused by the medicine he was taking for his piles. That night at Blackburn and the following night at Bolton he read with all his customary spirit. Early next morning they left for Blackpool. Dolby hoped that two days in Blackpool, with its invigorating sea air, would give Dickens the strength to get through the two remaining Readings of that week, in Preston on Thursday and in Warrington on Friday.

Beard's reply reached Dickens in Blackpool on Wednesday afternoon. He told Dickens that there could be no mistaking the symptoms. The medicine could not possibly have caused them. He recognised indisputable evidence of overwork and he wanted to treat him without delay. By Wednesday Dickens was feeling better. He wrote to Beard: "The said symptoms have greatly moderated since Sunday; but they are all *on the left side*. Six weeks will carry me through the Readings, if you can fortify me a little bit, and then, please God, I may do as I like." But he was impressed by the urgency of Beard's letter and thought it best to telegraph to him his addresses in Preston and Warrington.

They left Blackpool for Preston at mid-day on Thursday, 22 April. When they arrived Dickens went straight to the Bull Hotel, while Dolby called in at the Guildhall to see how the tickets were going for the Reading that evening. Every seat had been sold and the receipts were nearly two hundred pounds. He hurried to the hotel to give Dickens the good news, thinking it might cheer him. He found him standing in front of the fire in his sitting room holding a telegram. He handed it to Dolby without a word. It was from Beard. Dickens's letter from Blackpool had made him decide to come at once. He was already on his way and would arrive at Preston at half-past three that afternoon.

The train was an hour late and while waiting for Beard to arrive, Dickens wrote to Forster: "Tomorrow night at Warrington I shall have but 25 more nights to work through. If he can coach me up for them, I do not doubt that I shall get all right again – as I did when I became free in America." As soon as Beard arrived he gave Dickens a thorough examination. When he was finished they joined Dolby in the sitting room. Beard said to Dolby: "If you insist on Dickens taking the platform tonight, I will not guarantee but that he goes through life dragging a foot after him."

Tears were rolling down Dickens's face. He crossed the room to Dolby saying how sorry he was for all the trouble he was giving him. It was now five o'clock and the doors opened at seven. Dolby would have to leave at once to cancel the Reading. Dickens turned to Beard and said that Dolby could not possibly manage to let the ticket-holders know so late in the day. He asked to be allowed to read on that night at least, but Beard would not permit it.

Dickens and Beard left immediately for London. Dolby remained in Preston to announce the cancellation. To prevent out-of-town people from coming in for the Reading, he arranged with the station master to telegraph all railway stations within a radius of twenty miles that Dickens had been suddenly taken ill and would not read that night and that money would be returned the next day. For people travelling in by road, the Chief Constable dispatched mounted policemen along all roads leading to Preston. Every carriage coming in that direction was stopped and the occupants told. The next day the Mayor assisted Dolby at the return of money at the Guildhall. Very few of the disappointed ticket-holders complained and many expressed to Dolby their sympathy for Dickens in his illness.

In London Dickens was given a further medical examination by Beard, this time in consultation with Sir Thomas Watson, Both doctors agreed that he had been on the brink of an attack of paralysis of his left side and possibly of apoplexy. They signed a medical certificate which stated: "Mr. Charles Dickens has been seriously unwell, through great exhaustion and fatigue of body, consequent upon his public Readings and long and frequent railway journeys. In our judgment, Mr. Dickens will not be able with safety to himself to resume his Readings for several months to come." The Farewell Tour was at an end.

9

THE RACE IS OVER

Dickens had forced himself through seventy-four of the hundred Readings, the identical number which in America had brought him so near to collapse. It was now obvious to his friends that long before this his strength had been severely overtaxed, but he had deceived them all until it was too late. By travelling over the country, walking with a light step on to the platform and conjuring up a whole wonderful world of imaginary characters, he had succeeded in creating a fatal illusion about himself – that he was not ill.

He had deluded not only his friends but also himself. Sir Henry Thompson had diagnosed the pain in his foot as gout. Dickens told him that he had "an inward conviction" that it was not gout. He hated the idea of having gout and so he simply refused to have it. He told Forster: "I make out so many reasons against supposing it to be gouty, that I really do not think it is." He was delighted when Mr. Syme, the Edinburgh surgeon, said that the complaint originated in walking in snow. After his collapse, his friends marvelled at the extent of his self-delusion. Yates wrote: "He has pain, inflammation, every possible gouty symptom in his foot, the chosen locality for gout, but it is *not* gout, it is something originating in cold. The same symptoms appear in the other foot – still not gout. As he walked along the street one day, he could read only the halves of the letters over the shop doors that were on his right as he looked. 'He attributed it to medicine,' says Forster. It is really almost too astonishing!"

On the brink of an attack of paralysis of the left side after the Leeds Readings, Dickens again attributed the symptoms to the medicine he was taking. When Beard declared that the medicine could not possibly have caused them and that he recognised indisputable signs of overwork, Dickens could still ask him to "fortify" him sufficiently to complete the tour. Even as Beard, alarmed by Dickens's condition, was hurrying to Preston, Dickens was expressing the hope that the doctor could "coach" him up for the rest of the Readings.

What made Dickens behave in this way? He must have known that by continuing with the Readings as long as he did he was taking great risks with his health. He had shown, in other circumstances of his life, that he was not without foresight and discretion. He was, of course, reluctant to disappoint his public and he had a high sense of duty towards them. He had also a belief in hard work and perseverance. He had written much of this side of his nature into the character of David Copperfield: "Whatever I have tried to do in life, I have tried with all my heart to do well; whatever I have devoted myself to I have devoted myself to completely; in great aims and in small I have always been thoroughly in earnest." But to have continued the Readings under such circumstances could hardly be justified as the course of duty; it was foolhardy and headstrong.

There is, however, another character in *David Copperfield*, as frivolous as David is serious, as reckless as David is prudent, and that is Steerforth. There was as much of Dickens in Steerforth as there was in David, and during the Farewell Tour the Steerforth side of his nature was in the ascendant. Steerforth, with his handsome head thrown back and the freshness of the sea-wind on his face, saying, "Ride on! Rough-shod if need be, smooth-shod, if that will do, but ride on! Ride on over all obstacles and win the race!" "And win what race?" asks David. "The race that one has started in," says Steerforth. "Ride on!"

Then there were the Readings themselves, which had come to mean so much to him. It was not only to earn a large sum of money in a short space of time that he undertook the Farewell Tour so soon after his return from America. He was reluctant to discontinue reading. Only on the platform, under the hot lights, with an audience in front of him, could he feel himself again vibrating with his old zest for living. No other writer had ever identified himself so completely with the people. They showed their love for him every time he appeared on the platform and he needed their love. Only the Readings could keep at bay his ever-lengthening moods of depression. They distracted him from the thoughts on which he was constantly brooding: the degradation of his childhood, which had never ceased to haunt him; the failing of his literary powers; the separation from his sons; the decline of his superhuman energy and the approach of old age.

There was also the 'Murder'. Dickens himself placed this in a special category from all his other Readings. It had begun as a novelty to keep up receipts and to afford him, in this his Farewell Tour, a dramatic subject worthy of remembrance. But Dolby, that night in Edinburgh, had demolished the argument that the 'Murder' kept up receipts, by pointing out to Dickens that people would come to hear him for the last time whatever he read. This had enraged Dickens. Perhaps he was angry at the implication that he was not up to the work. He always resented any reference to his failing health. But this does not explain the extent of his anger. He was beside himself with rage. Dolby had never before seen him in such a temper. It is most probable that Dickens was angry because Dolby had taken from him any financial excuse for reading the 'Murder' so frequently.

There is no doubt that Dickens saw the 'Murder' as a piece of acting so powerful that people would speak of it long after his death and he was anxious to be remembered as one of the greatest actors of his day. But he could have achieved this by reserving the 'Murder', as Dolby had suggested, for a few of the large cities. He suffered terribly from the after-effects of the Reading and it is difficult to believe that he punished himself so severely and so frequently solely for the satisfaction of horrifying his audiences. There must have been some other reason.

At this time, when not travelling, he was living between Gad's Hill and the house of his mistress, Ellen Ternan. He was deeply unhappy. All these years after the separation he still could not bring himself to say a kind word about his wife. Little is known of his relationship with Ellen Ternan, but she does not seem to have given him any contentment. The 'Murder' Reading had become for him a means of expressing all the things he raged against in his mind, and as the ferocious blows rained down on the imaginary upturned face of Nancy, he was perhaps symbolically enacting his bitterness for his wife and his guilt over Ellen Ternan.

Reluctant as Dickens was to abandon the Farewell Tour, he had to heed, for a time at least, the stern warnings against continuing with the Readings expressed by Frank Carr Beard and Sir Thomas Watson. But just as he had refused to have gout, he also refused to believe that the Readings had been the cause of his breakdown. He blamed this entirely on excessive railway travelling. The Readings themselves had absolutely nothing whatever to do with it. Having convinced himself of this, he set about convincing others. He told Chappells: "The simple fact is, that the rapid railway travelling was stretched a hair's breadth too far, and that I ought to have foreseen it." He told Wills: "I had begun suddenly to be so shaken by constant Express travelling, that I might very easily have become ill." He told Percy Fitzgerald: "I am in brilliant condition, thank God. Rest and a little care immediately *unshook* the railway shaking." He told Fields: "I was too tired and too jarred by the railway fast express, travelling night and day." Always the railway travelling was to blame, never the Readings.

There was no doubt that excessive railway travelling had contributed greatly to his breakdown, but to blame it entirely on this was a deliberate refusal to face the facts.

In addition to his own desire to continue reading, Dickens was very concerned about the financial losses his breakdown had brought to Chappells. On 3 May he told Forster: "I do believe that such people as the Chappells are very rarely to be found in human affairs. To say nothing of their noble and munificent manner of sweeping away into space all the charges incurred uselessly, and all the immense inconvenience and profitless work thrown upon their establishment, comes a note this morning from the senior partner, to the effect that they feel that my overwork has been 'indirectly caused by them and by my great and kind exertions to make their venture successful to the extreme'. There is something so delicate and fine in this, that I feel it deeply."

Six weeks after his breakdown, Dickens asked Sir Thomas Watson if he might give twelve Farewell Readings in London only. He seemed so well that Watson did not think himself justified in refusing the request, but he stipulated that these Readings must not take place until the beginning of the following year and he strictly forbade all travelling in connexion with them. Dickens saw these Readings as a small compensation to Chappells.

His seemingly rapid recovery led many other people outside his immediate circle to believe that the doctors had exaggerated the dangers to his health, but his friends knew that the restrictions placed on him were absolutely necessary. They noticed that the old vitality was no longer there, except when he forced himself to make a special effort on their behalf, as he did that summer for his American friends, the Fields from Boston, and the Childs from Philadelphia, who were spending a holiday in Britain. Dickens wished to repay the kindness he had received from them in America and he arranged an elaborate programme of picnics and outings for their entertainment.

Dolby, who went down to Gad's Hill one weekend in June, was

surprised to see how well Dickens looked. He was very sunburnt and in his light suit of clothes, with his hat set jauntily on the side of his head, he seemed the picture of health. Dolby could hardly believe that this was the same man who had looked so desperately haggard and worn out only a few weeks previously.

Dickens had quickly resumed all his responsibilities. With Wills still absent, he was busy with the re-organisation of *All the Year Round*. Towards the end of July he began a new book to be entitled *The Mystery of Edwin Drood*. He resumed his extensive private correspondence. In September he went to Birmingham to deliver the Inaugural Address to the Midland Institute, of which he was president. Not only did he give an effective speech on the subject of education for the people but he promised to return in January to distribute the prizes to the students. His time was too fully occupied for a man who had recently escaped a dangerous illness.

By the third week in October he had finished the first number of *Edwin Drood*. He was also consulting with Dolby over every detail of the forthcoming Readings. He was at Gad's Hill until the end of the year working on the book, which he wanted as far forward as possible before the Readings began. This, of all times, was to be the only occasion in his reading career when he subjected himself to the strain of a series of Readings at the same time when he was writing a book. By the end of December the symptoms of April had returned; his left foot was painful and his sense of touch uncertain. When he went to Forster's house on New Year's Eve to read the second number of *Edwin Drood*, his friends noticed that he walked with difficulty.

To avoid railway travel he closed Gad's Hill for the duration of the Readings and rented a house at Hyde Park Place, near the Marble Arch. Early in January he moved there with Mamie and Georgina. But a few days before the Readings commenced he endured the agony of a railway journey when he went, as he had promised, to Birmingham on 6 January to distribute the prizes at the Midland Institute. He admitted to Forster that the journey had shaken him, but claimed to be in "good heart" for the Readings.

The London Farewell Readings began at the St. James's Hall on Tuesday, 11 January, 1870. The series of twelve was to include an afternoon Reading of *Sikes and Nancy*. This was to be given for the benefit of actors and actresses, who had difficulty in attending performances at night. The request for a special performance had come from the theatrical profession itself and this pleased Dickens enormously. The Readings began in an atmosphere of uncertainty and dread. Chappells were anxious. So far as they knew Dickens had undertaken these Readings solely to offset some of the losses caused to them by the cancellation of the tour, but whatever they had lost they did not want Dickens to sacrifice his health for their interests. His family and friends were anxious. They feared a recurrence of his breakdown or worse. Because of his determination to go on with the Readings they could do nothing to prevent him, but they did at least ensure that medical attention would be immediately on hand. Frank Carr Beard was asked to be present at every Reading. He, in turn, asked Charley Dickens to be there. He told him: "I have had some steps put up at the side of the platform. You must be there every night, and if you see your father falter in the least, you must run and catch him and bring him off to me, or, by Heaven, he'll die before them all."

Throughout the Readings Beard sat by the side of the platform. He noted the rate of Dickens's pulse before and after each Reading and so provided an exact record of the strain and pressure Dickens was undergoing. Dickens's normal pulse on the first night was 72, but on any subsequent night it was never lower than 82 and on later nights it had risen to more than 100. The Reading of *Copperfield* on the first night brought it to 95. *Dr. Marigold* on the second night brought it to 99. During the first Reading of the 'Murder' on Friday, 21 January his pulse rose from 90 to 112.

As he wiped out the Readings one by one his excitement increased. *Little Dombey* on 8 February brought his pulse from 91 to 114. When he read the 'Murder' for the third time on 15 February he was determined to outdo himself. Just before he stepped from the cover of the screen to the reading desk, he said to Kent in a low voice, "I shall tear myself to pieces". By the end of the Reading his pulse had risen from 90 to 124. He had to be supported to his dressing room and laid on a sofa for fully fifteen minutes before he could utter a rational sentence. The final Reading of *Copperfield* on 1 March caused his pulse to rise again to 124. Dickens himself was astounded at this high rate and believed it was caused by the emotion he had felt in parting for the last time from the Reading which he had liked better than almost any of the others. The final Reading of the 'Murder' on 8 March brought his pulse from 94 to 120. At the last Reading of all on 15 March his pulse was already 108 when he went on to the platform and at the conclusion of the Reading it had risen only two beats to 110.

During one of the three last Readings Charley noticed that his father was unable to articulate "Pickwick" properly, saying "Pickswick", "Picnic", "Peckswicks", all sorts of names except the right one. But apart from such obvious signs of exhaustion Dickens probably in all his life had never read so well. On his return from America a certain coarsening in the effects of the Readings had been noticed, because over there he had read so often in very large halls, but the old delicacy was again evident. This was Dickens reading at the top of his form.

Hardly a day passed during this series of Readings that his friends did not notice some effect on him of the disastrous excitements at the St. James's Hall. When he visited Forster on 23 January his left hand was in a sling. On 7 February, when he spent his fifty-eighth birthday at Forster's, the hand had not improved and on 25 February, when he read to him the third number of *Edwin Drood*, it was still swollen and painful.

The Final Farewell Reading took place on Tuesday, 15 March. From the start of his professional reading career on 29 April, 1858 to the end Dickens had read 444 times. He had given 134 Readings under the management of Smith, 70 under Headland and 240 under Dolby. He had kept no accurate records of his profit from

M

the Readings under Smith and Headland, but he estimated it to be £12,000. His profit from the Readings given under Dolby came to nearly £33,000. This made a grand total of approximately £45,000, an average of more than £100 a Reading. These earnings accounted for almost half of the £93,000 value of his estate at the time of his death. Dickens's Public Readings were by far the most successful one-man show of the nineteenth century. The only other author-showman to come anywhere near him was his friend Albert Smith, from whom he had learnt the technique of showmanship. Smith's own show at the Egyptian Hall in Piccadilly had earned him £30,000.

In the twelve years of the Readings Dickens had barnstormed across Britain and America being greeted by idolatrous audiences wherever he appeared, but the Final Farewell Reading was the crowning triumph. There were 2,034 people in the hall and the receipts were £422. Long before the doors opened great crowds had gathered at the Regent Street and Piccadilly entrances. Every class of society from the aristocrat to the working man had come to say goodbye to Dickens. The numbers turned away could have filled the hall three times over.

The Readings were the *Carol* and the *Pickwick Trial*. These were the very best that could have been chosen. They had always been great favourites with audiences. Punctually at eight o'clock Dickens walked on to the platform, book in hand. The great audience rose to its feet and cheered him. He stood there smiling, waiting to begin. Kent has described this memorable Reading: "Not a point was lost. Every good thing told to the echo, that is, through the echoing laughter. Scrooge, Fezziwig, the Fiddler, Topper, every one of the Cratchits, everybody in 'The Carol', including the Small Boy who is so great at repartee, were all welcomed in turn, as became them, with better than acclamations. It was the same exactly with 'The Trial from Pickwick' – Justice Stareleigh, Serjeant Buzfuz, Mr. Winkle, Mrs. Cluppins, Sam Weller, one after another appearing for a brief interval, and then disappearing for ever, each of them a delightfully humorous, one of them in particular, the Judge, a simply incomparable impersonation." Then Dickens closed his book and the Readings were over for ever.

The audience stood cheering and applauding, then suddenly a great silence fell as Dickens, who for once had lingered on the platform, returned to the reading desk and spoke his final words.

He said that it would be hypocritical and unfeeling if he were to disguise that he closed this episode of his life with feelings of very considerable pain. For many years he had been reading his own books to audiences whose sensitive and kindly recognition of them had given him instruction and enjoyment in his art such as few men could have had. But nevertheless he thought it well now in the full tide of public favour to retire upon older associations, and in the future to devote himself exclusively to the calling which had first made him known. In a reference to the forthcoming publication of the first number of *Edwin Drood*, he said that in two weeks' time he hoped to enter their own homes with a new series of Readings at which his assistance would be indispensable; "but," he concluded, "from these garish lights I vanish now for evermore, with a heartfelt, grateful, respectful, affectionate farewell".

During the delivery of this speech he did not hesitate or falter, but the mournful modulation of the words "from these garish lights I vanish now for evermore" was to haunt the memory of everyone who heard them. There was a brief hush as he moved from the platform, then the thunderous applause halted him and brought him back. He kissed his hand to the audience and left the platform, never to return.

Three months of life remained to him and every moment was filled with activity. He pressed on with *Edwin Drood*. On 21 March, as he walked along Oxford Street on his way to read the fourth number at Forster's house, the same incident recurred that he had experienced on a previous occasion, of not being able to read more than the right-hand half of the names over the shops. He still had the old fixed belief that this was the effect of the medicine he was taking for his piles.

On 5 April he spoke at the Annual Dinner of the Newsvendors Benevolent and Provident Institution. He apologised for the shortness of his speech. He said that he would try like Falstaff less to speak himself than to be the cause of speaking in others. "Much in this manner they exhibit at the door of a snuff-shop the effigy of a Highlander with an empty mull in his hand, who, apparently having taken all the snuff he can carry, and discharged all the sneezes of which he is capable, politely invites his friends and patrons to step in and try what they can do in the same line."

The last time he spoke in public was on 30 April, at the Royal Academy Dinner, where he returned thanks for "Literature". He was suffering intensely with his foot at the time and went solely to render a public tribute to his old friend Maclise, the painter, who had died three days previously. His appearance at the Academy Dinner led people to believe that he was not ill. A spate of invitations followed, some of which he felt obliged to accept. He dined with the American Ambassador. He dined at Lord Stanhope's. He breakfasted with Gladstone. This succession of engagements laid him up and he was unable to accompany Mamie to the Queen's Ball on 17 May. He had also to excuse himself from the dinner of the General Theatrical Fund, where the Prince of Wales was to preside. But a week later pressure was put on him to attend a dinner at Lord Houghton's, in order that the King of the Belgians and the Prince of Wales might meet him. When he got there he could not climb the stairs and the King and the Prince came down to him.

At the end of May he returned to Gad's Hill for the peace he could not obtain in London and which he needed for the completion of *Edwin Drood*. Dolby saw him for the last time on Thursday, 2 June at the office of *All the Year Round*. Dickens had travelled up from Gad's Hill that day to deal with the details of the periodical which needed his attention. He was so absorbed in business matters that Dolby rose to leave earlier than he had intended. When Dickens accompanied him to the door, Dolby noticed the difficulty of his walk and the agony in his face. He was troubled that he was leaving his Chief in pain, but he knew that Dickens would not like him to speak of it. They shook hands and parted without a word on either side.

Katey Dickens saw her father for the last time on Monday, 6 June. When she came down to breakfast he had already gone to the chalet in the garden to write. She had to go to London that day and would not return until Saturday. While waiting for the carriage that would take her to the station, she had an uncontrollable urge to see her father. She ran across the garden to the chalet. His head was bent over his work and he turned an eager and flushed face towards her. Usually he merely raised his cheek for a kiss, but this morning he pushed back his chair, opened his arms and took her into them. She hurried back to the house, saying to herself, without knowing why, "I am so glad I went. I am so glad."

On that Monday evening Dickens walked to Rochester to post his letters. On Tuesday he drove with Georgina to Cobham Wood. He dismissed the carriage and together they walked round the park and back. In the evening he put up some new Chinese lanterns, which had arrived from London that afternoon. He sat late with Georgina in the dining room admiring their effect when lighted. He spoke of his pleasure at renouncing London for Gad's Hill.

He spent the morning of Wednesday, 8 June writing in the chalet. He continued writing after lunch, which was not his usual habit. He was picturing a summer day in Rochester, where everything animate and inanimate was proclaiming the existence of God. "Changes of glorious light from moving boughs, songs of birds, scents from gardens, woods and fields – or, rather from the one great garden of the whole cultivated island in its yielding time – penetrate the Cathedral, subdue its earthy odour, and preach the Resurrection and the Life. The cold stone tombs of centuries ago grow warm; and flecks of brightness dart into the sternest marble corners of the building, fluttering there like wings."

He had ordered dinner for six o'clock, for he intended walking in the lanes afterwards. Dinner was begun before Georgina noticed the pain and trouble in his face. She was immediately alarmed. He told her that for an hour he had been very ill, but he wished dinner to go on. He then spoke disconnectedly of a sale at a neighbour's house, whether Macready's son was with his father at Cheltenham, of his own intention to return to London immediately. He had risen from the table and would have fallen where he stood had not Georgina supported him. She tried to get him to a sofa, but he was too heavy for her and she had to lower him to the floor, where he sank heavily on his left side. "On the ground," he murmured faintly. These were the last words he spoke.

Servants laid him on the sofa. The doctors were summoned and came that night. Nothing could be done. It was apoplexy. They judged it safer not to move him and he lay on the sofa breathing stertorously until ten minutes past six on the evening of Thursday, 9 June, when he died.

The following Tuesday Percy Fitzgerald entered Westminster Abbey leaving outside a hot sultry day. He walked into the cool vault through which a great crowd was filing silently past a handsome oak coffin fringed with white and red roses. Gazing down at the coffin, with its plain inscription, CHARLES DICKENS, he thought how *bright* the name looked.

APPENDIX

A NOTE ON THE READINGS

Professional Readings
Immediately after the Final Farewell Reading on 15 March, 1870, Dickens's friend, Charles Kent, suggested to him that an accurate record should be made of all the Readings given. Dickens approved and allowed Kent to examine all the relevant statistics. Kent's record, however, proved to be less than accurate and Walter Dexter set out to correct the errors and omissions. Dexter's lists of Readings, published in *The Dickensian*, volumes 37–39, come to a total of 427 Readings.

Unaccountably Dexter missed out 4 Readings given in Glasgow between the 3rd and the 6th December, 1861, and 13 Readings given in London in the spring of 1863. This brings the total to 444 Readings.

Of these, 370 were given in Britain and 74 in America. George Dolby, Dickens's manager, gives a total of 76 American Readings in his book *Charles Dickens as I Knew Him*. But Dolby records 4 Christmas Readings in Boston when in fact only 2 were given.

Charity Readings
Throughout his professional career as a reader Dickens continued to give charity Readings and Dexter's total of 26 would seem to be accurate.

Unperformed Readings
Twenty-one Readings were prepared by Dickens, of which

sixteen were given publicly. The Readings prepared but not performed were:

The Bastille Prisoner, from *A Tale of Two Cities*, serialised in *All the Year Round*, 30 April–26 November, 1859.

Mrs. Lirriper's Lodgings, from the Christmas number of *All the Year Round*, December, 1863.

The Haunted Man, from the Christmas story published in 1848.

Great Expectations, from the novel serialised in *All the Year Round*, 1 December, 1860–3 August, 1861.

The Signalman, from *Mugby Junction*, a collection of tales, published in the Christmas number of *All the Year Round*, December, 1866.

BIBLIOGRAPHY

Blom, Eric, Editor. *Grove's Dictionary of Music and Musicians.* Fifth Edition. Vol. VII. "St. James's Hall". Macmillan, 1954.

Dexter, Walter. "Mr. Charles Dickens Will Read", *The Dickensian*, Vols. 37–39. 1941–43.

Dickens, Charles. *The Letters of Charles Dickens.* Edited by Walter Dexter. Nonesuch Press, 1938.

The Letters of Charles Dickens. Edited by Madeline House and Graham Storey. Pilgrim Edition. Oxford, Clarendon Press, 1965–(In Progress) Vol. 1. 1820–39. Vol. 2. 1840–41.

Mr. and Mrs. Charles Dickens: His Letters to Her. Edited by Walter Dexter. Constable, 1935.

Mrs. Gamp. A Facsimile of the Author's Prompt Copy. Foreword by Monica Dickens. Introduction and Notes by John D. Gordan. New York, The New York Public Library, 1956.

Readings from the Works of Charles Dickens. With an Introduction "Charles Dickens as a Reader" by John Hollingshead. Chapman & Hall, 1907.

Sikes and Nancy: a Reading. With an Introduction and a General Bibliography of the Reading Editions by John Harrison Stonehouse. Henry Sotheran, 1921.

Dickens, Charles, Jr. "Reminiscences of My Father". *Windsor Magazine.* Supplement. December, 1934.

Dictionary of American Biography.

Dictionary of National Biography.

Dolby, George. *Charles Dickens as I Knew Him.* T. Fisher Unwin, 1885.

Field, Kate. *Pen Photographs of Charles Dickens's Readings.* Boston, James R. Osgood, 1871.

Fields, James T. *In and Out of Doors with Charles Dickens.* Boston, James R. Osgood, 1876.

Fitzgerald, Percy. *Memories of Charles Dickens*. Arrowsmith, 1913.

Fitz-Gerald, S. J. Adair. *Dickens and the Drama*. Chapman & Hall, 1910.

Forster, John. *The Life of Charles Dickens*. With Notes and an Index by A. J. Hoppé. 2 Vols. Dent, 1966.

Frith, William Powell. *My Autobiography and Reminiscences*. 3 Vols. R. Bentley, 1888.

Garis, Robert. *The Dickens Theatre: a Reassessment of the Novels*. Oxford, Clarendon Press, 1965.

Grimaldi, Joseph. *Memoirs of Joseph Grimaldi*. Edited by Charles Dickens. Fitzroy Edition. Macgibbon & Kee, 1968.

Hartnoll, Phyllis, Editor. *The Oxford Companion to the Theatre*. Second Edition. Oxford University Press, 1965.

Johnson, Edgar. *Charles Dickens: His Tragedy and Triumph*. 2 Vols. Gollancz, 1953.

Johnson, Edgar and Johnson, Eleanor, Editors. *The Dickens Theatrical Reader*. Gollancz, 1964.

Kennethe, L. A. "The Unique Reading Books". *The Dickensian*. Vol. 39. 1943.

Kent, Charles. *Charles Dickens as a Reader*. Chapman & Hall, 1872.

Lehmann, Rudolph Chambers. *Memories of Half a Century*. Smith, Elder, 1908.

Ley, J. W. T. *The Dickens Circle*. Chapman & Hall, 1918.

Macready, William Charles. *The Diaries of William Charles Macready*. Edited by William Toynbee. 2 Vols. Chapman & Hall, 1912.

Payne, Edward F. *Dickens Days in Boston*. Boston, Houghton Mifflin, 1927.

Pemberton, T. E. *Dickens and the Stage*. G. Redway, 1888.

Pope-Hennessy, Una. *Charles Dickens*. Chatto & Windus, 1947.

Ray, Gordon N. *Thackeray*. 2 Vols. Oxford University Press, 1955–58.

Rowell, George. *The Victorian Theatre*. Oxford, Clarendon Press, 1956.

Scott, Clement and Howard, Cecil. *The Life and Reminiscences of E. L. Blanchard*. 2 Vols. Hutchinson, 1891.

Storey, Gladys. *Dickens and Daughter*. Frederick Muller, 1939.

Tomlin, E. W. F., Editor. *Charles Dickens 1812–1870: a Centenary Volume*. Containing "Dickens and the Theatre" by Emlyn Williams. Weidenfeld and Nicolson, 1969.

Van Amerongen, J. B. *The Actor in Dickens*. Cecil Palmer, 1926.

Wilson, Edmund. *The Wound and the Bow*. Containing "Dickens: the Two Scrooges". W. H. Allen, 1941.

Woollcott, Alexander. *Mr. Dickens Goes to the Play*. Putnam, 1922.

Yates, Edmund. *His Recollections and Experiences*. Richard Bentley, 1885.

INDEX